KRISHNA JA

*HeartSmart*™

FLAVOURS OF

# *India*

HEART
AND STROKE
FOUNDATION
OF CANADA

DOUGLAS & McINTYRE
VANCOUVER/TORONTO/NEW YORK

Douglas & McIntyre
2323 Quebec Street, Suite 201
Vancouver, British Columbia
Canada v5t 4s7
www.douglas-mcintyre.com

*National Library of Canada Cataloguing in Publication Data*
Jamal, Krishna, 1939–
    HeartSmart flavours of India

    ISBN-13: 978-1-55054-612-5 · ISBN-10: 1-55054-612-0

    1. Low-fat diet—Recipes. 2. Cookery, India. I. Heart and Stroke Foundation
of Canada. II. Title. III. Title: Heartsmart flavours of India.
TX724.5.I4J38 1998    641.5′638′0954    C97-911043-2

Editing by Elizabeth Wilson
Cover design by Peter Cocking
Text design by Isabelle Swiderski
Photography by John Sherlock
Photography assistance by Alastair Bird
Food styling by Nathan Fong
Tableware provided by Chintz & Co., Vancouver
Drawings by Michela Sorrentino
Printed and bound in Canada by Friesens
Printed on acid-free paper
Distributed in the U.S. by Publishers Group West

The publisher gratefully acknowledges the assistance of the Canada Council and of the British Columbia Arts Council. The publisher also acknowledges the financial support of the Government of Canada through the Book Publishing Industry Development Program and the Province of British Columbia through the Book Publishing Tax Credit for its publishing activities.

*Cover photo: Steamed Salmon in Banana Leaf, p. 89*

# Contents

# Acknowledgments

*Building a HeartSmart cookbook that offers the South Asian community of Canada as well as the general Canadian market the opportunity to enjoy the flavour wonders of Indian cooking has been a challenge met by a great team of people:*
HSF, Canada—Bill Tholl, Executive Director; Doug MacQuarrie, Director, Health Promotion; members of the Health Promotion Initiatives Review Committee.
HSF, B.C. & Yukon—Richard Rees, Executive Director; Fiona Ahrens, Director, Marketing and Communications.

*Sincere thanks also go to:*
    Ursula Fradera, M.Sc., R.D. for her project management and her guidance on many nutritional aspects of the book; Isabeau Iqbal for her analysis of the recipes; Rosie and Avtar Singh for their recipe testing; Consulting Nutritionist Supriya Gupta, B.Sc., R.D., for her concept input and nutrition advice on the recipes and manuscript; South Asian health educator Bridget Awatramani for her community perspective; Swati Scott, R.D. for her manuscript review; Leanne Johnson, B.A. for her editorial input; Carol Dombrow, B.Sc., R.D. for her ready advice; Scott McIntyre and his team at Douglas and McIntyre; the staff of Rubina Tandoori for their support; Krishna Jamal, master of an amazing palette of flavours!

*The Heart and Stroke Foundation*


Thanks to my assistant, Ranjeet Sandhu, who helped me develop recipes. She also cooked them on her own and let my family try—a good test to make sure they were easy to understand. My dear friend Sushma Dutt also offered many helpful suggestions during our "bharta Saturdays."
    My appreciation to the people at the Heart and Stroke Foundation of Canada: Fiona Ahrens, for assisting in every possible way; Ursula Fradera, for all her work as project manager, Isabeau Iqbal, for working weekends to do the analysis and Supriya Gupta and Bridget Awatramani from Toronto for ideas and recipe input.
    I have to thank my mother, Mrs Savitri Champsi and my mother-in-law, Mrs Gulshakar Jamal. Both of these confident cooks shared their knowledge with me. My two sons have helped in their way. Shaffeen insisted that only the best should go in the book, Farid signed me up as one of the pioneering restaurants in the HeartSmart Restaurant Program. Lastly I have to thank my husband, Amin, for getting me started.

*Krishna Jamal*

# Preface

Heart disease and stroke—they affect more Canadians than any other disease. The wonder that is the multicultural face of Canada is also present in disease statistics. Research also shows that we all, from every ethnic background, have the power to make a difference to those statistics with simple everyday healthy choices, beginning with the food we prepare.

For the past seven years the Heart and Stroke Foundation of Canada has reflected this in its cookbook publishing program with titles such as:

- *The Lighthearted Cookbook,* Anne Lindsay
- *Lighthearted Everyday Cooking,* Anne Lindsay
- *Simply HeartSmart Cooking,* Bonnie Stern
- *More Simply HeartSmart,* Bonnie Stern
- *HeartSmart Chinese Cooking,* Stephen Wong

These books are creatively and carefully assembled to offer mouthwatering recipes, a complete nutritional analysis of each one and a nutrition preface to guide you in the general direction of healthy meal-making.

We are proud to introduce the second in our New World of Cooking series, *HeartSmart Flavours of India.* Chef Krishna Jamal takes us on an exotic journey into simple, flavour-filled, healthy dishes. I hope you enjoy the adventure!

*Audrey Vanderwater*

Audrey Vanderwater
President, Heart and Stroke Foundation of Canada

The South Asian Community Council is delighted to have taken part in the development of this cookbook. The Heart and Stroke Foundation has long recognized the need to support our community in the challenge of combating the very high rates of heart disease amongst South Asians.

We have the power to make a difference in the choices that we make—every day, right in our own kitchens. *HeartSmart Flavours of India,* featuring the flavour magic and innovation of chef Krishna Jamal, will certainly give me, and I hope many others, an opportunity to rethink how we cook old favourites and how to try wonderful new dishes. A dedicated team of people have put a huge amount of creativity, nutrition testing and recipe development into this book. Now it is up to us to begin making a difference.

*Priya Suppal*

Dr Priya Suppal
President, South Asian Community Council
Heart and Stroke Foundation of Ontario

Supriya Gupta, R.D.(Registered Dietitian). As an active member of the South Asian Community Council and one of the original inspirations for this book, Supriya continued to advise on its development and creation. She runs a lipid clinic in Toronto, specializing in high cholesterol, diabetes, weight loss and general nutrition, and has appeared on the Life Television Network's *Body Break.*

Bridget Awatramani, B.A., another member of the original concept team, is well known in the South Asian community as a health promoter and nutritionist. In her teaching and writing she focuses on international cooking and heart-healthy living for seniors. She is also active in the S.A.C.C.

*The South Asian Heart Health Network (SAHHN) brings together government, professional and voluntary agencies to cooperate in heart health initiatives targeted at ethnic Asian communities. Currently there are networks in Canada, U.S.A., U.K., India, Pakistan and Singapore. In Canada, for more information contact Dr Arun Chockalingam, (613) 954-8651.*

# Introduction

The sign outside our restaurant says "Rubina Tandoori—Lazeez Cuisine of India." "Lazeez? What part of India is that from?" our customers ask. The answer is, all over. "Lazeez" simply means "tasty." Indian food is delicious no matter where it's from, and it varies considerably from one place to another. I have spent a good part of my life travelling, tasting and talking in order to discover the secrets of Indian regional specialties, so that I can offer the widest possible sampling to my guests and students—and now, to you.

I began cooking professionally in London, England. Our first restaurant served typical English food when we bought it. I couldn't help but add a little ginger here or a bit of chili there. We gradually introduced Indian dishes, and within a year we had a successful Indian restaurant.

One restaurant led to another. In London, the Indian people come from everywhere, so I was constantly experimenting and questioning as I tried to create "their" dishes from home. To this day, everywhere my family and I go, India and beyond, we investigate the Indian food and then work to re-create it.

My experiments must have worked. Our restaurant in Vancouver has received wonderful accolades from magazines, guidebooks and newspapers. And at the request of many of our guests, I've also started cooking classes, to show people the simple techniques I use.

In 1992 I was encouraged to develop recipes that would fit the guidelines of the Heart and Stroke Foundation's HeartSmart Restaurant Program. More experimentation, with the result that Rubina Tandoori was one of the first Indian restaurants in Canada to participate.

So come, explore and experiment with me. If you're new to Indian cooking, don't let the variety of spices intimidate you. Almost all of them, including the spice mixes (masalas) are available in your supermarket. You might want to make your own spice mixes too, with my tried-and-true masala recipes. In these recipes you can drop any one spice and the food will still taste wonderful. And whether a recipe is mild or hot, feel free to add or subtract some chilies.

If you're already cooking Indian food and want to cook HeartSmart, with less fat and salt, you may find some dishes with a different taste angle but, if our restaurant patrons are any judge, they're still delicious.

Enjoy this book, and may all your cooking be *lazeez*.

*Krishna Jamal*
Executive Chef, Rubina Tandoori

You can visit our restaurant on the Web at www.rubina.com. For any questions about cooking techniques, e-mail me at krishna@rubina.com.

For questions about nutrition, contact your regional Heart and Stroke Foundation at 1-888-HSF-INFO or on the Web at www.hsf.ca.

# HeartSmart Eating
## THE INDIAN WAY

Why Indian cooking? India and the subcontinent are an ancient region where the love of good food runs deep. Basic Indian ingredients are wholesome and delicious, with extensive use of fruits and vegetables, whole grains, legumes and dairy products. India has a large population of vegetarians, and a wealth of history to draw from in developing and preparing the nutritious and lower-fat dishes that conform to HeartSmart criteria. Meat servings are generally small. Bread is made fresh daily, using mostly whole grains. Yogurt is often a major ingredient. Add to all that the aromatic spices that deliciously flavour each dish, and Indian cooking becomes a palette of flavours and textures.

Although generally the emphasis is on whole grains, vegetables and legumes, Indian cooks often deep-fry, and liberally use *ghee* (clarified butter) and high-fat dairy products such as cream and whole milk. Chef Krishna Jamal has done wonders in redesigning traditional Indian recipes to use HeartSmart ingredients and cooking techniques while still keeping the fascinating flavours.

### VARIETY—THE ESSENCE OF INDIAN COOKING

A typical Indian meal is a combination plate, or *thali* (a large round plate), with several small dishes providing an assortment of tastes, textures and colours that will ignite all your senses. You may find a vegetable dish or two, a meat, chicken or fish dish, a *daal* (lentil dish), bread and/or rice, chutneys and pickles, yogurt and some fruit or, occasionally, sweets. Can this many dishes still be HeartSmart? Yes! Variety is the spice of life, and also the key to good nutrition.

The recipes in *HeartSmart Flavours of India* were created with today's cook in mind. You can design your own HeartSmart thali combination or you can serve one or two dishes as part of a Western meal. The emphasis is on choice and variety. Simple serving suggestions and a complete nutritional analysis will help you create delicious and nutritious Indian dishes.

Indian cooking techniques are remarkably easy; they suit our hectic lives. The key is to prepare most of your ingredients ahead of time. Spices are gently toasted to enhance their delicate flavours; the remaining ingredients are then added fairly quickly. After that you can usually take your time, as Indian dishes are left to cook gently for a long time to bring out the flavours. So let's get cooking! You'll be amazed by how easy it is to prepare a dazzling array of dishes.

## THE WONDERFUL WORLD OF SPICES

Traditional Indian cuisine combines herbs and spices in infinite ways to create unique flavours. Standard spice mixes are known as *masalas*—literally, "mixtures." You can mix your own with Krishna's basic masala recipes (p. 5) or buy them at any major supermarket or Indian market.

Adding herbs and spices to dishes, and reducing the need for salt, is one of our delicious HeartSmart cooking secrets. Most Canadians eat more sodium (salt) than their bodies need. Excessive sodium intake can lead to high blood pressure in salt-sensitive individuals.

You'll soon find that herbs and spices add taste and variety to very simple dishes. With little effort, you'll create some intoxicatingly aromatic, colourful and tasty dishes—the HeartSmart way.

## BREADS AND GRAINS

Canada's Food Guide to Healthy Eating recommends 5 to 12 servings of grain products a day, and no Indian thali would be complete without rice or freshly made bread. Bread is more popular in the North and rice is more common in the South. We've brought the North and South together by providing you with plenty of recipes for both.

Breads are the foundation for the multitude of tastes and textures in Indian cooking. Indian breads use whole grains, beans, rice or lentils, which provide carbohydrates, fibre, B-vitamins and iron.

Because of the Mogul influence, traditional breads are made in *tandoors* (clay ovens) or on *tavas* (griddles). Chef Krishna has adjusted recipes to suit the Western kitchen. She has also substituted ghee with vegetable oil, or eliminated it altogether. These bread recipes are lower in fat and salt than the traditional versions and still taste just as wonderful.

Many people don't know that rice went to China from India, not the other way around! This grain is so central to Indian life that it is used in many religious ceremonies (throwing rice at western weddings comes from India), and is an important component of any celebratory meal. Imagine how Cumin Rice (p. 21) or Lemon Rice (p. 22) can add a new spirit to your dinner.

Basmati rice is used most often in Indian cooking. Available in both white and brown varieties, basmati rice has a light and delicious nutty flavour. These recipes use white basmati rice, but you could substitute brown basmati, regular brown long-grain rice or a combination for an even more nutritious meal.

*Bean Cooking Timesaver*
• When you cook beans, make a large batch
• Cook uncovered for required time
• Press them between your fingers to see if they are done
• Store them in a self-sealing bag in small portions and freeze them
Now you are ready to go for your next delicious bean recipe and you don't have to buy the more expensive canned beans.

## MEAT, POULTRY AND FISH

While meat is not the emphasis of an Indian meal, it *is* served in combination with other dishes. Small amounts of meat are consumed in bite-sized pieces, like Chicken Tikka (p. 71), or in flavourful stews, like Traditional Lamb Curry (p. 66). A balanced, nutritious diet includes meat. To be HeartSmart, choose leaner cuts, eat smaller portions and remove the skin from poultry.

The Moguls of Persia introduced meat to India and brought with them the tandoor oven to cook it in. Tandoori Chicken (p. 84) is the result of the Mogul influence, and a favourite dish worldwide. Like all poultry cooked in India, Tandoori Chicken is traditionally cooked without the skin, which in turn, considerably reduces the total fat content.

Fish is a mainstay along the coasts of India. Try the spicy Madras Prawns (p. 92) or Fish Vindaloo (p. 90). Fatty fish, such as salmon, mackerel and trout, contains omega-3 fatty acids which scientists believe might play a role in preventing the formation of blood clots and therefore may lower your risk for heart disease.

## BEANS AND THINGS

With a traditionally large population of vegetarians, India has a rich and varied history of vegetarian cooking. India is the world leader in the production of dried beans, peas and lentils, with more varieties than you can name. These are high in protein and can be quickly turned into incredible dishes. They can be mashed (Chickpea Dip, p. 110), sprouted (Bean Sprout Salad, p. 17) or ground (Chickpea Pancake, p. 101). And no traditional thali would be complete without a daal (stewed bean or lentil dish), even in meat-eating households. You can serve daal as a light entree, a soup or as a meal in itself. Just add more or less water to create your perfect daal.

With so much variety, it's easy to follow the suggestion of Canada's Food Guide to Healthy Eating to eat peas, beans and lentils—dried or canned—more often.

## A FLAVOUR ZIP TO VEGETABLES AND FRUITS

An array of vegetables and fruits is reflected on our HeartSmart thali, served alone or alongside other dishes. Some vegetables are pureed (Roasted Eggplant, p. 39), others are quickly stir-fried (Balti Vegetables, p. 38), and all of them are delicately spiced to enhance their natural taste.

Fruit is usually served fresh in Indian cuisine. You'll find fruit sliced on the thali, added to yogurt to make refreshing drinks like the popular

Lassi (p. 124), or combined in a Fascinating Fruit Salad (p. 15). It is also preserved in the form of pickles or chutneys.

However you serve them, fruits and vegetables are rich in nutrients, particularly minerals and vitamins. Try to include bright red and orange fruits and vegetables (carrots, squash, mangoes) and dark leafy greens (spinach, broccoli) in your dishes more often. They contain beta carotene and other antioxidants that might help prevent heart disease and cancer.

### DAIRY PRODUCTS IN THE INDIAN DIET

Indians love dairy products, and having them available is a symbol of wealth and prosperity. Dairy products and eggs are the only sources of vitamin B-12 for lacto-ovo vegetarians. Chef Krishna has adapted traditional higher-fat dairy products with lower-fat alternatives, so you can enjoy these dairy delights without upsetting your daily fat budget.

No thali would be complete without a yogurt dish, served hot in soup like Kadhi (p. 13) or cold in Raita (p. 112). Sweetened yogurt makes a refreshing drink, like Mango Lassi (p. 124). However you serve it, yogurt is easily digested and it provides protein, calcium and other nutrients. Its cooling tang also counteracts hot spices. Chef Krishna uses low-fat or nonfat yogurt, which can be drained to make rich-tasting, creamy textured Low-fat Thick Yogurt (p. 112).

Indian cheese, or *panir,* is another popular but traditionally high-fat favourite. It can be an appetizer, entree or even a dessert. There's a low-fat recipe for Panir on page 50, but if you don't have time to make it, you can substitute tofu in recipes like Spinach and Cheese, or *Saag Panir* (p. 50).

You won't find *ghee,* (clarified butter) on our HeartSmart thali. It is, of course, high in both total and saturated fat. Most of these recipes use a little bit of vegetable oil, lowering the total fat and saturated fat in the dishes. When you see butter in a recipe, it's important for texture, and it's included under HeartSmart serving guidelines.

### THALI CONDIMENTS

Chutneys and pickles are usually used as an appetizer dip or served with a meal to add further variety and spice to the thali. These Indian equivalents of Western relishes or salsas will add excitement to the simplest meals.

Chutneys can either be preserved or served as fresh salsas. Pickles use preserving liquids such as vinegar or salted water, but again, can be served fresh or put in jars to mature. Chef Krishna provides the busy cook with two quick pickle recipes on pages 104–5. Believe it or not, there's even a Coconut Chutney

*Vegetable Boost*
**Most Indian meals include a few slices of raw vegetables with a tiny sprinkling of salt and a squeeze of lemon juice. These vegetable relishes are an easy way to add vegetables to a Western meal too.**

recipe (p. 108). These condiments are lower in salt, fat and sugar than store-bought ones, and are easy to make. We encourage you to try them out.

## SWEET TREASURES

Sweets are not a common component of Indian cooking, but small quantities of them do make their appearance on special occasions and religious celebrations. Try Krishna's Carrot Halva (p. 115), or a new take on Rice Pudding (p. 119) for a sweet and nutritious dessert and a wonderful way to round out your meal.

Drinks play a big part in the Indian diet because of the hot climate. Cold drinks tend to contain some salt to help prevent dehydration and replenish minerals. In this book the salt content is reduced and whole milk and yogurt are replaced with their low-fat or nonfat counterparts.

## TRY IT!

We wish you an exotic journey, whether you choose to add only a dish or two to a Western meal or go all out and put together a HeartSmart thali.

*Supriya Gupta and Ursula Fradera, Registered Dietitians*

### Nutrient Analysis

Nutrient analysis of the recipes was performed by Registered Dietitian Isabeau Iqbal, using the Food Processor® Nutrition Analysis Software, Version 6.03 (ESHA Research, 1995) software program. The nutrient database was the 1991 Canadian Nutrient File, supplemented when necessary with documented data from reliable sources.

The analysis was based on
  • Imperial weights and measures
  • first ingredient listed when there was a choice of ingredients
Canola oil and homemade unsalted stocks were used throughout.

Specific measures of salt were included in the analyses, but "salt to taste" was not. Use the least salt that you find acceptable. Optional ingredients and garnishes in unspecified amounts were not calculated.

### Nutrient information on recipes

Nutrient values have been rounded to the nearest whole number. Non-zero values less than 0.5 are shown as "trace."

Good and excellent sources of vitamins (A, C, E, B6, B12, thiamine, niacin, riboflavin, folacin) and minerals (calcium, iron and zinc) have been identified according to the RNI criteria (highest value of range was the standard). (*Guide to Food Labelling and Advertising*, Agriculture and Agri-food Canada, 1996).

A serving that supplies 15% of the Recommended Daily Intake (RDI) for a vitamin or mineral (30% for vitamin C) is a good source of a nutrient. An excellent source must supply 25% of the RDI (50% for vitamin C).

A serving providing at least 2 g of dietary fibre is considered a moderate source. Serving providing 4 g and 6 g are high and very high respectively. (*Guide to Food Labelling and Advertising*, Agriculture and Agri-food Canada, 1996).

# The Pantry

# The Pantry

Welcome to the world of Indian food. The recipes in this book range from simple to sophisticated. Even if you're new to my kind of cooking, there are recipes here that will become old friends. Surprise your palate with an Indian-spiced hamburger, or some barbecued marinated fish chunks. Spice up your plate with an onion-y fresh vegetable relish. Change your whole attitude to rice, beans and lentils with some simple but intensely flavoured preparations. It's easier than ever to add a little bit of India to your plate.

───────────────── THE QUICK PICK PANTRY ─────────────────

**With these basic spices and flavourings you can prepare most of the delicious recipes in this book:** *cardamom, cinnamon, cloves, coriander, cumin, mustard seeds, peppercorns, turmeric, red chili powder, canned crushed tomatoes, fresh ginger and garlic.* **You can also save time by keeping a selection of** *canned beans and lentils, and some plain low-fat yogurt.*

SPICES, HERBS AND FLAVOURINGS

Indian cooking makes an art of combining, blending and balancing spices and herbs—within a dish and within a meal—to create a glorious variety of tastes.

**Hot they're not!**

Spices don't necessarily equal heat. Only a few spices make food spicy-hot, and you can avoid or reduce those when you cook for yourself. When my recipes call for a certain number of chilies, there's the reminder: "or to taste."

Even without the hot spices, these recipes will create dishes with layers of exquisite flavour—and cut down on the need for too much salt or fat.

**Aniseed** *(Saunf):* These tear-shaped seeds of the anise plant have a sweet, pungent, licorice flavour. They're widely used in Bengali- and Kashmiri-style dishes, either whole or ground. Fennel seeds taste somewhat similar and can be used as a substitute.

**Asafoetida** *(Hing):* This is the dried sap of a plant native to Afghanistan and Iran. It is available in its original resinous form, but ground asafoetida is much more convenient. Because its strong, almost medicinal taste doesn't appeal to everyone, I consider it an optional ingredient.

**Cardamom** *(Elaishi):* If you've ever enjoyed the Indian pistachio-and-

Ingredient photo, p. 12

almond ice cream, *kulfi*, you've tasted cardamom. This fragrant spice comes as whole or ground seeds or as woody, oval pods with one pointed end. It's best to buy pods and remove the seeds if you need them. Green and white cardamom are subtle and fine flavoured. Black cardamom is stronger.

**Carom seeds** *(Ajowan):* These tiny seeds are used in savoury dishes and pickles. The flavour is an interesting combination of licorice and dill, but they also impart heat. There's no real substitute so they're considered optional.

**Chilies** *(Mirch):* Heat and flavours vary from one variety of chili to another, so buy with your own taste in mind. Chilies can be used fresh or dried, whole, ground into powder or preserved in one of the thousands of colourfully labelled hot sauces and chili pastes on the market.

**Cilantro** *(Dhania, Chinese parsley, fresh coriander):* The refreshingly pungent leaves of the coriander plant are sold in bunches, like parsley. The fresh flavour is lost in cooking, so cilantro should always go in at the last minute.

**Cinnamon** *(Dalchini):* From the Mediterranean to China, cinnamon is found in both sweet and savoury recipes. It is the dried inner bark of a small evergreen tree. Cinnamon comes ground or in "sticks."

**Cloves** *(Laung):* These nail-shaped dried flower buds are used in both sweet and savoury dishes—whole baked ham studded with cloves is a classic North American example. Cloves are available whole or ground.

**Coriander seeds** *(Dhania):* From these pale round seeds we get an important element in the *masalas* or spice mixtures of Indian cooking. Generally, coriander is mixed with cumin to make it more subtle. This combination, called Dhania-jeera (p. 6), makes the most basic mild curry powder. Coriander is available whole or ground. The seeds taste nothing like the fresh leaves, which are known as cilantro.

**Cumin** *(Jeera):* Cumin's elongated seeds impart a warm, slightly smoky flavour with licorice overtones. Whole, ground, or combined with other spices, it plays a big part in the cooking of India, Mexico and the Middle East.

**Curry leaves:** Native to India, curry leaves are used fresh or dried to flavour savoury dishes. Don't confuse them with curry powder, nor with the leaves of the ornamental "curry plant." The real curry leaves are available fresh in Asian shops and dried in shops catering to Indians. In some recipes I use bay leaves as a substitute, in others curry leaves are considered optional.

**Fennel seeds** *(Saunf):* These curved greenish seeds have a subtle licorice flavour, with no bitterness. They're a familiar component of Italian cooking, particularly Italian sausage. Fennel seeds are generally bought whole and used either raw or toasted.

*Hot Spices*
**This chili symbol indicates a dish that is traditionally fiery. Chilies, carom seeds, ginger and peppercorns are the spices that impart heat, and you can reduce the heat in recipes by reducing, or even eliminating them, particularly chilies.
As far as spicy heat goes, these recipes are moderate by Indian standards.**

**Fenugreek seeds** *(Methi seeds):* These small hard golden rectangles are powerful in aroma and flavour. They're usually toasted before use to neutralize bitterness. They go very well with eggplant and potatoes, and are also added to mixtures that will ferment, to prevent them from going off. The seeds are used whole or ground.

**Fenugreek leaves** *(Kasuri methi):* The slightly bitter leaves of the fenugreek plant are often served as a vegetable in Indian cooking. These mid-green, slightly serrated ovals come three to a stem. They can be found in bunches in Asian markets. Dried leaves in packages can be found in Indian shops. These have the aroma of sweet hay. Dried leaves should be picked over to remove sticks, or ground to a powder.

**Ginger** *(Adarak):* This knobby, pale brown rhizome is one of the mainstays of Asian cooking. Its unmistakable hot/sweet flavour adds excitement to both sweet and savoury dishes. You can buy ground ginger, but in most recipes fresh is preferable.

**Mace** *(Javitri):* The shell of a nutmeg has a lacy red membrane around it which tastes and smells much like nutmeg, only more subtle. Mace is usually sold in ground form. Nutmeg can be used as a substitute if you reduce the quantity by half. Mace is a natural preservative.

**Mango powder** *(Amchoor):* This tart beige powder is often used in place of lemon juice to impart sourness. Made from dried unripe mangoes, it's rich in vitamin C.

**Mint** *(Podina):* Mint's cooling freshness is a pleasant complement to hot and spicy dishes. The leaves can be used fresh or dried. It's usually available with the fresh herbs in the produce section.

**Mustard seeds** *(Rai):* The familiar processed mustard is made from mustard seeds. You can find these seeds whole or ground. The white mustard seeds found in pickling spices are milder than the black seeds often called for in Indian cooking, but either one works. They're used in savoury dishes.

**Nutmeg** *(Jaiphal):* In North America the warm, piquant flavour of nutmeg is favoured for baking and sprinkling on eggnog. In India, its affinity with other spices makes nutmeg an important element of spice mixes. The whole nutmeg keeps very well and is easy to grate, but ground nutmeg is available too.

**Saffron** *(Kesar):* The most expensive spice, but the most spectacular also, saffron comes in threads which are the dried stigmata of the saffron crocus. It's used for flavouring and colouring sweet and savoury dishes. To add colour evenly, soak saffron in a little hot water before adding to a dish. Mexican saffron is much cheaper than the best, Spanish saffron, but you must use much more to get the same intensity. There is no flavour equivalent of saffron, but if it's only the golden colour you're after, use food colouring.

**Star anise:** This flower-shaped collection of woody pods consists of (usually) eight "petals," each containing a shiny brown seed. The pods are more flavourful than the seeds so the spice is used whole or in sections. This spice has an anise flavour, and aniseeds can be substituted, but the quantity should be increased slightly.

**Tamarind** *(Imli):* Tamarind is used to add a unique sourness to chutneys, stews and drinks. It is actually the pulp from the pods of the tamarind tree, and it's available as a paste or in compressed blocks (often with seeds). Both are available in Asian stores. Tamarind is a major component of Worcestershire sauce.

**Turmeric** *(Haldi):* Turmeric is a member of the ginger family, and its rhizome provides a bright golden savoury spice used in most curry powders.

## MASALAS—FLAVOUR MAGIC

Here are recipes for some of the classic Indian masalas, or spice mixtures. You can easily find commercial brands of these in Indian stores and in most supermarkets.

### Meat Masala

This rich mixture adds excitement to meat and poultry dishes.

| | | |
|---|---|---|
| 6 tbsp | coriander seeds | 90 mL |
| 3 tbsp | cumin seeds | 45 mL |
| ½ tsp | carom seeds (optional) | 2 mL |
| ¼ | star anise (2 to 3 sections) | ¼ |
| 3-inch | cinnamon stick | 8 cm |
| 4 | cloves | 4 |
| 3 | cardamom pods, preferably black | 1 |
| 4 to 5 | bay leaves | 4 to 5 |
| 1½ tsp | dried cilantro | 7 mL |
| ½ tsp | mace | 2 mL |
| 1½ tsp | ground turmeric | 7 mL |
| 1½ tsp | powder red chili | 7 mL |

*Spicier Spices*
**Always buy spices in small quantities, as they lose their flavour after sitting for too long. Store them in airtight containers and keep in a cool place away from light—even in the freezer. I recommend buying whole spices and grinding them as you need them because whole spices last much longer. An electric coffee grinder or the small jar of a blender works best.**

*Dhania-jeera Masala*

Here's a simple mixture that is lovely in vegetables. A mild curry powder is the commercial equivalent.

| | | |
|---|---|---|
| 7 tbsp | coriander seeds | 100 mL |
| 4 tbsp | cumin seeds | 60 mL |

*Sabzi Masala*

This spice mix makes vegetables and seafood come alive.

| | | |
|---|---|---|
| 2 tsp | Dhania-jeera Masala | 10 mL |
| entire recipe | Meat Masala | entire recipe |

*Garam Masala*

This famous masala provides a delicious final touch to spicy meat and chicken curries, as it is added at the very end of cooking.

| | | |
|---|---|---|
| 4 tbsp | ground cinnamon | 60 mL |
| 1 tbsp | ground cloves | 15 mL |
| 1 tbsp | ground cardamom | 15 mL |
| 1 tsp | ground mace | 5 mL |

1. Heat large heavy unoiled skillet (preferably with no non-stick coating) over low heat. Add whole spices and toast, tossing occasionally until fragrant. (Do not toast ground spices or leaves. Combine these with whole spices later.)
2. Let toasted spices cool, then grind in clean electric coffee grinder or small jar of blender. Stir in powdered spices and store in airtight containers away from heat and light.

## BEANS, PEAS AND LENTILS

If you love the sweet, smoky taste of pea soup or the layers of heat and spice in a chili con carne, you have some idea of the infinite potential of dried beans, peas and lentils.

These dried legumes, collectively known as "pulses," provide carbohydrates, protein, fibre and often iron. They are a vital part of the diet of the millions of vegetarians in India, and they augment the small amounts of meat in the cooking of non-vegetarians.

Indian spices turn these humble staples into taste sensations. Pulses show up at any meal, and in thousands of guises. They're so much a part of the cuisine that Indians are real bean and lentil connoisseurs, and are particular about which kind they use in which dish.

In North America you can find a full range in Indian stores, and often in health food stores. But feel free to substitute whatever beans and lentils you have on hand. There are many kinds readily available in supermarkets.

**When is a bean . . . a lentil?**

The Hindi word *daal* literally means "leguminous." In this book I translate "daal" as "lentil"—that means it refers to split peas and split beans as well as to true lentils. Here is a guide to the beans and daals you will find in these recipes.

**Chickpeas** *(Chole, kabli chana, garbanzo beans):* These large round yellow beans have a mild flavour and firm texture. They are available canned or dried. Because of their size, dried chickpeas should be soaked overnight, then boiled for at least 16 minutes before simmering to remove gas-causing compounds.

**Chickpea lentils** *(Chana daal):* Treat these the same as whole beans. Bread flour of ground chickpea lentils is called channa flour or *besan*.

**Kidney beans** *(Rajma):* These flavourful red beans get their name from their shape. They are available canned or dried. As with chickpeas, the dried ones must be soaked overnight then boiled for at least 16 minutes before simmering.

**Mung beans** *(Moong beans):* These are the green-skinned, yellow-fleshed beans used for Chinese bean sprouts. They are tender and tasty when cooked and need very little pre-soaking.

**Mung bean lentils** *(Moong daal):* Split mung beans can be found with or without the green skin.

**Pigeon pea lentils** *(Toor daal, tuvar daal, arhar daal):* These round yellow lentils are made from husked and split dried pigeon peas. They thicken in response to lemon or lime juice. They're available in Indian and Latin American stores and often in supermarkets.

**Red lentils** *(Masoor daal):* These tiny pinkish-red split peas turn yellow after cooking and have a nutty taste. They are very convenient because they needn't be soaked before cooking. Rinse them well and they're ready.

**Indian black beans** *(Urad beans, mah beans):* These small, cylindrical black beans are an Indian variety and bear no resemblance to the black-skinned beans from North America. Because their texture becomes creamy when cooked, substituting other lentils will affect the texture of the dish. Look for them in Indian or health food stores.

**Indian black bean lentils** *(Urad daal, mah daal):* These are dusty white, with no black skin. They're often ground to make flour for breads.

*Cooking Beans and Lentils*

**Pre-soaking beans and lentils begins the water absorption, but also releases many of the compounds that cause gas. Soaking-water is discarded to get rid of them, unless the lentils will be ground and fermented. Those compounds that make a fermenting dough double in size are the same ones you discard with the soaking-water!**

**Start beans, peas and lentils in boiling water, and boil the largest ones for at least 16 minutes, to release further gas-producing compounds, before simmering.**

*Look in the index under "Appetizers" for a list of great Indian starters.* **There's no chapter for appetizers and starters in this book because a dish can appear as an appetizer one day and as part of a light meal another day. It all depends on the serving size.**

## THE INDIAN MEAL

We Indians like to have a choice of dishes for our meals, and the variety on our table surpasses all other cuisines. There's usually a small appetizer to start, two or three main dishes, a bread of some sort and rice. There are some pickles and relishes, a plate of sliced vegetables sprinkled with salt, pepper and lemon juice, and a dessert of fresh fruit, or occasionally a pudding. This may sound like a lot, but we eat just a little from each dish. Each recipe in this book can be served as part of a Western meal, but if you'd like to experience a HeartSmart all-Indian meal, here are some suggested combinations.

*Satisfying but not heavy*
Bengali fish, plain basmati rice, Balti vegetables (dry-spiced mixed vegetables) and mint chutney

*Cold winter's day dinner*
Traditional lamb curry, hot broccoli soup, mixed vegetables, chapati and plain basmati rice

*Vegetarian selection*
Two vegetable dishes of choice, curried chickpea lentils (channa daal), raita, chapati, plain basmati rice and almond fudge.

*Luxury Sunday dinner*
Lamb pulao, fascinating fruit salad (fruit chaat), quick vegetable pickle (sambharo), raita, fresh tomato relish (tomato cachumbar) and rose milk pudding

*Light supper*
Chickpeas and potatoes (aaloo chole), chicken or lamb kebab, plain rice, chapati, mango chutney and lassi of choice

*Leisurely dinner with friends*
Cumin chicken, paratha or naan bread, Afro-Indian spiced potatoes, grated cabbage and onion salad with tamarind-chutney-and-raita salad dressing and rose milk pudding.

# Soups & Salads

❭ *indicates hot dishes*

# Thick Lentil Vegetable Soup
## SAMBAR

*This lentil stew/soup gets its body from* toor daal, *lentils made from pigeon peas. These thicken in response to lemon or lime juice. If you can't find these, other lentils will do, but they won't thicken up in the same way. Sambar can be served with rice and bread. The South Indians prefer this soup on the side with the potato-stuffed crepes called* masala dosa *(p. 44) or the steamed rice bread,* idli *(p. 102).*

*Lentils:*

| | | |
|---|---|---|
| 1 cup | red or yellow lentils, preferably pigeon pea lentils (toor or tuvar daal) | 250 mL |
| 6 cups | water | 1.5 L |
| 1 tsp | salt | 5 mL |
| 1 tsp | ground turmeric | 5 mL |
| 1 tsp | crushed ginger | 5 mL |
| 1 tsp | crushed garlic | 5 mL |
| 1 tsp | vegetable oil | 5 mL |
| | | |
| 1 tbsp | vegetable oil | 15 mL |
| 2 to 4 | fresh or dried chilies, or to taste | 2 to 4 |
| 1 tsp | mustard seeds | 5 mL |
| ½ tsp | cumin | 2 mL |
| | a few curry leaves | |
| 1 | medium onion, chopped | 1 |
| 2 | medium tomatoes, diced | 2 |
| ½ cup | vegetable of your choice, chopped | 125 mL |
| 1 tsp | Sambar Masala (see facing page) | 5 mL |
| 2 tbsp | Tamarind Sauce (p. 109) or lemon juice | 25 mL |
| | cilantro | |

**EACH SERVING PROVIDES:**

| | | |
|---|---|---|
| | Calories | 165 |
| g | Protein | 10 |
| g | Carbohydrates | 24 |
| g | Fibre | 6 |
| g | Fat | 4 |
| g | Saturated Fat | trace |
| mg | Cholesterol | 0 |
| mg | Sodium | 368 |
| mg | Potassium | 471 |

Excellent: iron, fibre
Good: thiamine, vitamin E

1. Rinse lentils, cover with water and soak for 20 minutes. Drain. Boil 6 cups/1.5 L fresh water. Add lentils, salt, turmeric, ginger, garlic and 1 tsp/5 mL oil. Reduce heat to low and simmer for 1 hour or more (half the time for red lentils), or cook in pressure cooker for 35 to 40 minutes. Mixture will be quite thick. Set aside.
2. Heat oil in large pan over high heat. Add chilies, mustard and cumin seeds. When seeds start to pop, add curry leaves and onion. Cook for

2 minutes or until fragrant. Add tomatoes, vegetables, sambar masala and tamarind sauce or lemon juice. Cook until vegetables are tender.

3. Add cooked lentils and mix well. Bring to boil, remove from heat, garnish with cilantro and serve.

*Serves 6*

*Sambar Masala*

| | | |
|---|---|---|
| 2 tbsp | coriander seeds | 25 mL |
| 2 to 3 | dried red chilies | 2 to 3 |
| 1½ tsp | cumin seeds | 7 mL |
| ½ tsp | poppy seeds | 2 mL |
| ½ tsp | fenugreek seeds | 2 mL |
| ½ tsp | mustard seeds | 2 mL |
| 1½ tsp | yellow split peas | 7 mL |
| 1 tsp | fine unsweetened coconut | 5 mL |
| 3 | dried curry leaves or 2 bay leaves | 3 |
| ¼ tsp | ground cinnamon | 1 mL |
| ½ tsp | ground turmeric | 2 mL |

1. Toast seeds, split peas and coconut in unoiled pan over low heat. Toss around until fragrant.
2. Let toasted spices cool, add leaves and grind mixture in blender or clean electric coffee grinder. Mix in ground spices.

# Hot Broccoli Soup

1. basmati rice 2. see qua 3. red pepper 4. cilantro 5. mung beans 6. eggplant 7. ginger 8. bitter melon 9. okra 10. chickpea lentils 11. red chili powder 12. cumin seeds 13. red chilies 14. green chilies 15. garlic 16. black cardamom pods and seeds 17. curry leaves 18. cinnamon sticks 19. star anise

*Broccoli is Italian, not Indian, but I serve it to my family because it's an easy and enjoyable way to add calcium to our diets. In our restaurant I serve this soup to begin lunch, but for me broccoli soup and naan bread is lunch.*

*For a creamier texture, without cream, add mashed potato to the soup, or stir in low-fat yogurt just before serving.*

| | | |
|---|---|---|
| 1 | medium onion | 1 |
| 1-inch | piece ginger | 2.5 cm |
| ½ tsp | vegetable oil | 2 mL |
| 1 tsp | ground cumin | 5 mL |
| ½ tsp | red chili powder, or to taste | 2 mL |
| 2 cups | vegetable stock or water | 500 mL |
| 3 cups | water | 750 mL |
| ½ lb | broccoli florets, finely chopped | 250 g |

1. Thinly slice onion and finely grate ginger.
2. Heat vegetable oil in soup pot over high heat. Add onion and ginger and cook until golden brown. Stir in cumin and chili powder. Cook, stirring, for 2 minutes. Add vegetable stock and water and bring to boil. Add broccoli florets and boil covered for 10 minutes.
3. If you like smooth broccoli soup, puree in blender and gently reheat.

*Serves 4*

**EACH SERVING PROVIDES:**

| | | |
|---|---|---|
| | Calories | 28 |
| g | Protein | 2 |
| g | Carbohydrates | 6 |
| g | Fibre | 2 |
| g | Fat | trace |
| g | Saturated Fat | trace |
| mg | Cholesterol | 0 |
| mg | Sodium | 27 |
| mg | Potassium | 225 |

Excellent: vitamin C
Good: folacin

# Yogurt Soup
### KADHI

*Westerners use cream to make rich soups. But from time immemorial, Indians have used yogurt to achieve the same texture. The people from Gujarat use this soup as a base. Like many soups, this one is wonderful the next day. You can make it as a starting point and add any vegetables you like.*

| | | |
|---|---|---|
| 2 cups | low-fat yogurt | 500 mL |
| 2 tbsp | chickpea flour (channa flour) | 25 mL |
| 5 cups | water | 1.25 L |
| 2 tsp | vegetable oil | 10 mL |
| 2 | dried chilies, or to taste | 2 |
| 1 tsp | cumin seeds | 5 mL |
| 1 tsp | mustard seeds | 5 mL |
| 4 to 5 | curry leaves (optional) | 4 to 5 |
| 1 tsp | salt | 5 mL |
| 1 tsp | crushed ginger | 5 mL |
| 1 tsp | crushed garlic | 5 ml |
| ¼ tsp | ground turmeric | 1 mL |
| ½ tsp | red chili powder, or to taste | 2 mL |
| 1 tsp | Dhania-jeera Masala (p. 6) or mild curry powder | 5 mL |

1. In blender, combine yogurt, chickpea flour and water. Blend well and set aside.
2. Heat oil in heavy soup pot over high heat. Add dried chilies, cumin seeds, mustard seeds and curry leaves. When seeds begin to pop, add remaining ingredients. Cook for 2 minutes. Add blender mixture and bring to boiling point, stirring constantly. Reduce heat to low, continue stirring and simmer for 15 minutes. (If left unattended, it can boil over.) Serve immediately or reheat gently when ready to serve. Stands alone as soup or as sauce over rice as part of a whole meal.

*Serves 8*

From top right: Mango Lassi (p. 124), Five Lentils (p.32), Cauliflower and Potatoes (p. 40), Peas and Potatoes (p. 41), Basmati Rice (p. 20), Raita (p. 112)

*Yogurt*
**Yogurt is a great way to get your daily calcium. It's used extensively in Indian cooking, often made from high-fat buffalo milk. Nonfat yogurt, made from skim milk, has the same nutritional value as whole milk versions, but contains no fat. It's a good idea to drain off some of the liquid—it then becomes as rich-tasting as the high-fat yogurts (see p. 112).**

**EACH SERVING PROVIDES:**

| | | |
|---|---|---|
| | Calories | 67 |
| g | Protein | 4 |
| g | Carbohydrates | 6 |
| g | Fibre | 1 |
| g | Fat | 3 |
| g | Saturated Fat | 1 |
| mg | Cholesterol | 4 |
| mg | Sodium | 324 |
| mg | Potassium | 168 |
Good: vitamin B-12

# Spicy Potato Salad
## AALOO CHAAT

*Chaat literally means "snack." Chaats are India's fast food, sold at stalls clustered on the beaches of the Indian Ocean.*

| | | |
|---|---|---|
| 2 | large potatoes, boiled, skinned and coarsely chopped | 2 |
| 4 tbsp | Raita (p. 112) | 60 mL |
| ¼ tsp | red chili powder, or to taste | 1 mL |
| ¼ tsp | Chaat Masala (see below) | 1 mL |
| 2 | medium tomatoes | 2 |
| ½ cup | green onions, chopped | 125 mL |
| 1 tbsp | finely chopped cilantro | 15 mL |

1. Gently coat potatoes with raita. Divide into 4 serving bowls and sprinkle chili powder and chaat masala over each portion. Place tomatoes and onions on top and garnish with cilantro.

*Serves 4*

*Chaat Masala*

| | | |
|---|---|---|
| 2 tbsp | cumin seeds | 25 mL |
| 1 tbsp | black peppercorns | 15 mL |
| 1 tsp | carom seeds | 5 mL |
| 2 | cloves | 2 |
| 1 tbsp | dried mint | 15 mL |
| ½ tsp | black rock salt, or regular rock salt | 2 mL |
| 1 tsp | ground ginger | 5 mL |
| 2 tsp | mango powder | 10 mL |
| 1 tsp | red chili powder, or to taste | 5 mL |
| ¼ tsp | ground asafoetida (optional) | 1 mL |

1. Heat unoiled skillet over low heat. Toast cumin seeds, peppercorns, carom seeds and cloves until fragrant. Toss often to prevent burning.
2. Let toasted spices cool; grind in small, clean electric coffee grinder or small jar of blender. Mix with powdered spices.

*Fading Flavours*

**Once ground, spices will begin to lose their flavour. The amounts recommended in this book are based on freshly ground spice. Adjust to taste. To preserve flavours of ground spices, keep them away from light and heat—dark containers, dark cupboards, away from the stove. An excellent way to preserve flavours, especially if you don't use these spices all the time, is to keep them in airtight jars or tins in the freezer.**

# Chickpea Salad
## CHANNA CHAAT

*I think I have tasted the best chaats at Bombay's Juhu Beach, where 50 or so food stalls sell every combination you can imagine. Quite often, when there's a choice between buying chaats and walking home or getting a taxi home and eating there, Juhu Beach chaats win out.*

| | | |
|---|---|---|
| 14-oz | tin chickpeas, rinsed and drained | 398 mL |
| 1 | medium onion, coarsely chopped | 1 |
| 1 | medium tomato, diced | 1 |
| 4 tbsp | Low-Fat Thick Yogurt (p. 112) | 60 mL |
| 1 tsp | Chaat Masala (see facing page) | 5 mL |
| 4 tsp | Tamarind Sauce (p. 109) or balsamic vinegar | 20 mL |
| ½ cup | cilantro | 125 mL |

1. Mix chickpeas, onion and tomato. Divide into 4 servings.
2. Spread yogurt over top of each serving, sprinkle with chaat masala, spoon tamarind sauce over top and garnish with cilantro.

*Serves 4*

**EACH SERVING PROVIDES:**

| | | |
|---|---|---|
| | Calories | 219 |
| g | Protein | 12 |
| g | Carbohydrates | 37 |
| g | Fibre | 7 |
| g | Fat | 4 |
| g | Saturated Fat | trace |
| mg | Cholesterol | 1 |
| mg | Sodium | 143 |
| mg | Potassium | 492 |

Excellent: folacin, iron,
Good: phosphorus, zinc

# Fascinating Fruit Salad
## FRUIT CHAAT

*This is a recent discovery for me. My friends and I went to a sari shop on Main street in Vancouver where the staff were eating fruit chaat for lunch. They offered us some and we were amazed by how good it tasted. Now, in summer, this fruit salad has become a standard on my family menu.*

| | | |
|---|---|---|
| 1 lb | mixed fruit: honeydew, pears, apples, bananas, grapes, etc., diced | 500 g |
| 1 tsp | Chaat Masala (see facing page) | 5 mL |

1. In large bowl, mix fruit with chaat masala and serve.

*Serves 4*

**EACH SERVING PROVIDES:**

| | | |
|---|---|---|
| | Calories | 75 |
| g | Protein | 1 |
| g | Carbohydrates | 19 |
| g | Fibre | 2 |
| g | Fat | 1 |
| g | Saturated Fat | trace |
| mg | Cholesterol | 0 |
| mg | Sodium | 105 |
| mg | Potassium | 270 |

# Kidney Bean and Banana Salad
### FOOGATH

*Cooking bananas*

**Regular bananas are fine for cooking, but they do tend to become mushy. If you live in an area where there are lots of Asian and Indian shops, you may be able to find cooking bananas, a special variety of sweet bananas that hold up to cooking without breaking down. These are smaller and sweeter than plantains, the large starchy bananas used in savoury dishes.**

*On hot summer days, I get hungry very quickly if I eat green salad, but I feel lethargic if I eat something too heavy. I find this salad just right.*

| | | |
|---|---|---|
| 14-oz | tin kidney beans | 398 g |
| 2 | bananas | 2 |
| ½ | red pepper | ½ |
| 1 | tomato, preferably roma | 1 |
| 1 tsp | vegetable oil | 5 mL |
| 2 tsp | lemon juice | 10 mL |
| ¼ tsp | red chili powder, or to taste | 1 mL |
| ⅛ tsp | salt | 0.5 mL |

1. Rinse and drain beans.
2. Cut bananas into ½-inch/1 cm circles, slice red pepper, chop tomato into small pieces.
3. Heat oil over high heat. Add bananas and cook, gently stirring, until golden brown. Add beans, bell pepper, tomato, lemon juice, chili powder and salt and mix. Reduce heat to low and cook covered for 5 minutes. Cool and serve.

*Serves 4*

**EACH SERVING PROVIDES:**

| | | |
|---|---|---|
| | Calories | 73 |
| g | Protein | 1 |
| g | Carbohydrates | 16 |
| g | Fibre | 2 |
| g | Fat | 2 |
| g | Saturated Fat | trace |
| mg | Cholesterol | 0 |
| mg | Sodium | 72 |
| mg | Potassium | 317 |

Good: vitamin B–6, vitamin C

# Bean Sprout Salad

*Indian bean spouts aren't the same as Chinese bean sprouts, even though they're both made from mung beans. Indian ones have just barely sprouted. Germination takes about a day and a half, and directions are here in the recipe, but if you're in a hurry you can substitute the easy-to-find Chinese bean sprouts, for a slightly different taste.*

*If you don't like raw bean sprouts, saute them with thinly chopped garlic for a couple of minutes before adding to the salad.*

| | | |
|---|---|---|
| 1 cup | mung beans (moong beans) | 250 mL |
| ¾-inch | piece ginger | 2 cm |
| 1 | small cucumber | 1 |
| 1 | thin slice cantaloupe | 1 |
| 1 | green chili or banana pepper | 1 |
| ½ tsp | coarsely ground black pepper | 2 mL |
| ¼ tsp | salt | 1 mL |
| 2 tsp | lemon juice | 10 mL |

1. Rinse beans and soak overnight or 12 hours. Drain water, fold damp towel to surround beans and let germinate for 24 hours. Sprinkle water over towel if it has dried out. When beans have split and about ¼-inch/5 mm of sprout is visible, remove from towel. Rinse with cold water and drain. Put in salad bowl.
2. Grate ginger, dice cucumber and cantaloupe and thinly slice chili into wheels (remove seeds).
3. Add chili, pepper, ginger, lemon juice and salt to bean sprouts. Fold in cucumber and cantaloupe and chill for 30 minutes before serving.

*Serves 4*

## Bean Sprouts

**Sprouting substantially increases the vitamin content of peas and beans. And what a tasty way to increase your soluble fibre intake.**

**Fibre comes in two forms: soluble and insoluble. Soluble fibre (pulses, oat bran, oatmeal) is believed to lower cholesterol levels. Insoluble fibre (whole-grain foods, fruit and vegetables), with its water-retaining capacity, increases bulk and helps prevent and control bowel problems.**

### EACH SERVING PROVIDES:

| | | |
|---|---|---|
| | Calories | 152 |
| g | Protein | 10 |
| g | Carbohydrates | 29 |
| g | Fibre | 5 |
| g | Fat | 1 |
| g | Saturated Fat | trace |
| mg | Cholesterol | 0 |
| mg | Sodium | 139 |
| mg | Potassium | 517 |

Excellent: vitamin C, folacin
Good: thiamine

# Fresh Vegetable Relishes
## CACHUMBARS

*Raw vegetables or fruit, a pinch of spices, a squeeze of citrus, a scattering of herbs—these simple relishes add a burst of freshness to an Indian meal.*

*Mild onion is the essential ingredient in any cachumbar. After that you can add cabbage, carrots, cucumber, tomatoes and whatever else you wish. To make it tastier, I add sliced green chilies or red chili powder and lime or lemon juice. You can also use raita (p. 112) or tamarind sauce (p. 109). Be adventurous and try your own concoctions. Who knows? Maybe you'll come up with a recipe you want to share with me.*

**EACH SERVING PROVIDES:**

| | | |
|---|---|---:|
| | Calories | 33 |
| g | Protein | 1 |
| g | Carbohydrates | 7 |
| g | Fibre | 2 |
| g | Fat | trace |
| g | Saturated Fat | trace |
| mg | Cholesterol | 0 |
| mg | Sodium | 8 |
| mg | Potassium | 274 |

Excellent: vitamin C

*Tomato Cachumbar*

| 1 | small mild onion | 1 |
|---|---|---|
| 2 | ripe tomatoes, peeled | 2 |
| ½ | small cucumber | ½ |
| 1 | green chili, or to taste | 1 |
| 1 tsp | lemon juice | 5 mL |

**EACH SERVING PROVIDES:**

| | | |
|---|---|---:|
| | Calories | 17 |
| g | Protein | 1 |
| g | Carbohydrates | 4 |
| g | Fibre | 1 |
| g | Fat | trace |
| g | Saturated Fat | trace |
| mg | Cholesterol | 0 |
| mg | Sodium | 4 |
| mg | Potassium | 125 |

*Radish Cachumbar*

| 1 | small mild onion | 1 |
|---|---|---|
| 6 | large radishes | 6 |
| ½ | small cucumber | ½ |
| ½ | bunch cilantro, chopped | ½ |
| 1 to 2 tsp | lime juice | 5 to 10 mL |

**EACH SERVING PROVIDES:**

| | | |
|---|---|---:|
| | Calories | 41 |
| g | Protein | 1 |
| g | Carbohydrates | 10 |
| g | Fibre | 2 |
| g | Fat | trace |
| g | Saturated Fat | trace |
| mg | Cholesterol | 0 |
| mg | Sodium | 9 |
| mg | Potassium | 231 |

*Mango Cachumbar*

| 1 | small mild onion | 1 |
|---|---|---|
| ½ | underripe mango, peeled | ½ |
| 2 | tomatoes | 2 |
| 1 tbsp | chopped cilantro | 15 mL |
| pinch | red chili powder | pinch |
| 2 tsp | wine vinegar | 10 mL |

1. Quarter onions, cut fruits and vegetables coarsely, slice chilies in half and remove seeds (optional).
2. In mixing bowl, combine all ingredients and serve.

*Serves 4*

# Rice & Pasta Dishes

❩ *indicates hot dishes*

# Basmati Rice

*Basmati rice, grown in North India and Pakistan, is considered the King of Rice by many Asian people. Its nutlike flavour and delicate fragrance are attributed to the soil in which it grows. You can substitute any other long-grained white rice—it requires the same cooking time—but you won't get that genuine Indian flavour.*

| 2 cups | basmati rice | 500 mL |
| 4 cups | water | 1 L |
| ½ tsp | salt | 2 mL |
| ¼ tsp | lemon juice | 1 mL |

## Method 1

1. Rinse rice until water runs clear. Cover rice with warm water and soak at room temperature for 20 minutes. Drain.
2. In ovenproof pot, bring 4 to 5 cups/1 to 1.25 L fresh water to boil with salt and lemon juice. Add rice, cover and boil on high heat for about 10 minutes or until rice starts to soften.
3. Reduce heat to medium and simmer covered until all water is absorbed, about 20 minutes.
   Or, after rice has started softening, cook covered in preheated 300°F/150°C oven for 15 minutes, or cook covered at full power in microwave for 5 to 6 minutes. Cover rice with damp cloth and pot lid to prevent drying out.

## Method 2

1. Rinse rice until water runs clear. Cover with warm water and soak rice at room temperature for 20 minutes. Drain.
2. Over high heat, bring 8 to 10 cups/2 to 2.5 L fresh water to boil with 1 tsp/5 mL salt and ¼ tsp/1 mL lemon juice. Add rice, return to boil, then reduce heat to medium. Simmer uncovered for 15 to 20 minutes. When rice is soft but not mushy, remove from heat and drain.
3. Reheat before serving by microwaving, covered, on high power for 5 minutes. Rice done this way will not be sticky.

See photo facing p. 13

*Serves 6*

# Cumin Rice

*This is my childhood favourite. My mother is a very good cook—so good that we never knew this dish was made of leftovers. I like it so much that now I make it from scratch. It's fun to eat because the cumin seeds are untoasted when you put them in, so when you eat one you get a burst of cumin flavour.*

| | | |
|---|---|---|
| 2 cups | long-grain rice | 500 mL |
| 1 tbsp | vegetable oil | 15 mL |
| 1 | cinnamon stick | 1 |
| 2 | cloves | 2 |
| 2 | cardamom pods | 2 |
| 2 tsp | cumin seeds | 10 mL |
| 4 cups | water | 1 L |
| 1 tsp | lemon juice | 5 mL |
| 1 tsp | salt | 5 mL |

1. Rinse rice until water runs clear. Cover and soak in warm water for 20 minutes. Drain.
2. Preheat oven to 350°F/180°C, unless you will be microwaving.
3. Heat oil in ovenproof pot over high heat. Add cinnamon stick, cloves and cardamom pods. When spices start to pop, add cumin seeds and water and bring to boil. Add rice, lemon juice and salt. Cover, return to boil, reduce heat to low and cook for 10 minutes. Rice will still be moist.
4. Cover rice with damp cloth and pot lid. Transfer to oven and bake for 15 minutes, until moisture is gone and rice grains are separate. Or microwave, covered, on high power for 4 minutes and serve.

*Serves 4*

**EACH SERVING PROVIDES:**

| | | |
|---|---|---|
| | Calories | 403 |
| g | Protein | 8 |
| g | Carbohydrates | 83 |
| g | Fibre | 1 |
| g | Fat | 5 |
| g | Saturated Fat | 1 |
| mg | Cholesterol | 0 |
| mg | Sodium | 543 |
| mg | Potassium | 27 |

# Lemon Rice

*My first encounter with lemon rice was in a Bengali restaurant in London, England. It's a traditional Bengali dish. Try it with fish dishes, particularly fish vindaloo (p. 90) and Bengali fish (p.87).*

| | | |
|---|---|---|
| 2 cups | basmati or other long-grain rice | 500 mL |
| 1 tsp | vegetable oil | 5 mL |
| 1 tsp | mustard seeds | 5 mL |
| 2 | bay leaves | 2 |
| 1 | green chili (or to taste), stemmed and halved | 1 |
| 4 cups | water | 1 L |
| 1 tsp | salt | 5 mL |
| 2 tsp | lemon juice | 10 mL |

1. Rinse rice and soak in warm water for 20 minutes. Drain and set aside.
2. Preheat oven to 350°F/180°C, unless you will be microwaving or simmering.
3. Heat oil in heavy ovenproof pot over high heat. Add mustard seeds, bay leaves and green chili. When seeds start to pop, add water, salt and lemon juice. Bring to boil; add rice and boil covered for 10 minutes.
4. Cover rice with damp cloth and pot lid. Transfer to oven and bake for 10 minutes. Or microwave on high power for 4 minutes. Or simmer (without damp cloth) over low heat for 10 minutes.

*Serves 4*

**EACH SERVING PROVIDES:**

| | | |
|---|---|---|
| | Calories | 382 |
| g | Protein | 8 |
| g | Carbohydrates | 82 |
| g | Fibre | 1 |
| g | Fat | 3 |
| g | Saturated Fat | 1 |
| mg | Cholesterol | 0 |
| mg | Sodium | 540 |
| mg | Potassium | 10 |

# Pulao Rice

*Pulao rice was developed to use up leftover vegetables. But the recipe is so good that the original purpose is long forgotten and people now make it on purpose. Any cachumbar relish (p. 18) goes very well with this.*

| | | |
|---|---|---|
| 2 cups | basmati or other long-grain rice | 500 mL |
| 6 to 8 cups | water | 1.5 to 2 L |
| ½ tsp | lemon juice | 2 mL |
| 1 tsp | salt | 5 mL |
| 1 tbsp | vegetable oil | 15 mL |
| 1 | medium onion, chopped | 1 |
| 1 tsp | cumin seeds | 5 mL |
| ¼ tsp | crushed ginger | 1 mL |
| ¼ tsp | crushed garlic | 1 mL |
| 1 | green chili (or to taste), sliced | 1 |
| ¼ cup | diced pepper | 50 mL |
| ½ cup | frozen corn or mixed vegetables | 125 mL |
| ½ cup | chopped green onions for garnish | 125 mL |

1. Rinse rice until water runs clear, cover with warm water and soak for 20 minutes. Drain.
2. In large ovenproof pot, over high heat, bring 6 to 8 cups/1.5 to 2 L fresh water to boil with lemon juice and salt. Add rice, cover and boil for 10 minutes. Rice will still be slightly hard. Drain.
3. Preheat oven to 350°F/180°C, unless you prefer to microwave.
4. In skillet, heat oil over high heat. Add onion and cook until soft. Add cumin seeds and cook for 2 minutes or until fragrant. Add ginger, garlic, chili, pepper and corn. Saute for 5 minutes or until vegetables are tender. Remove from heat and fold into rice.
5. Cover rice with damp cloth and pot lid and bake in preheated oven for 15 minutes. Or transfer to microwavable covered dish and microwave for 5 minutes. Garnish with green onions and serve.

*Serves 4*

**EACH SERVING PROVIDES:**

| | | |
|---|---|---|
| | Calories | 436 |
| g | Protein | 9 |
| g | Carbohydrates | 91 |
| g | Fibre | 2 |
| g | Fat | 5 |
| g | Saturated Fat | 1 |
| mg | Cholesterol | 0 |
| mg | Sodium | 546 |
| mg | Potassium | 167 |

Excellent: vitamin C

See photo facing p. 85

# Sweet Rice
## ZARDA

*This is very nice on its own, but it's normally eaten with very spicy dishes.*
*Try it with a beef or fish vindaloo (p. 62, p. 90) or Madras prawns (p. 92).*

| | | |
|---|---|---|
| 1½ cups | basmati rice | 375 mL |
| 1½ tsp | butter | 7 mL |
| 1½ tsp | vegetable oil | 7 mL |
| 2 | cardamom pods | 2 |
| 1-inch | cinnamon stick | 2.5 cm |
| 2 | cloves | 2 |
| 2½ cups | water | 625 mL |
| 7¾-oz | tin crushed pineapple in its own juice | 220 g |
| pinch | saffron or a few drops | pinch |
| | yellow food colouring (optional) | |
| ½ cup | sugar | 125 mL |
| 1 tbsp | almond flakes | 15 mL |
| 1 tsp | halved pistachio nuts | 5 mL |
| 1 tbsp | raisins | 15 mL |

1. Rinse rice until water runs clear, cover with warm water and soak for 20 minutes. Drain.
2. Preheat oven to 350°F/180°C
3. Heat butter and vegetable oil in large ovenproof pot and add cardamom, cinnamon and cloves. Add 2½ cups/625 mL fresh water and bring to boil. Add rice, cover and return to boil. Reduce heat to medium and simmer until rice is half-cooked (about 15 minutes). Dissolve saffron in pineapple juice. Stir pineapple, juice, sugar, nuts and raisins into rice.
4. Cover rice with damp cloth and pot lid. Bake covered for 20 minutes and serve.

*Serves 4*

**EACH SERVING PROVIDES:**

| | | |
|---|---|---|
| | Calories | 431 |
| g | Protein | 6 |
| g | Carbohydrates | 90 |
| g | Fibre | 3 |
| g | Fat | 5 |
| g | Saturated Fat | 1 |
| mg | Cholesterol | 4 |
| mg | Sodium | 30 |
| mg | Potassium | 184 |

Excellent: thiamine, iron
Good: vitamin E

# Creamy Saffron Sauce for Pasta

*My husband's friend Vincenzo persuaded me to try Italian/Indian fusion cuisine. I have combined pasta with Indian spices in this tasty dish.*
*Fettuccini works well here. For best flavour, boil the pasta until just cooked, then drain and add it to the sauce to cook gently for a few minutes.*
*Seafood is excellent with this sauce.*

| | | |
|---|---|---|
| 2 cups | 2% milk | 500 mL |
| pinch | saffron | pinch |
| 2 to 3 | bay leaves | 2 to 3 |
| 1 tsp | vegetable oil | 5 mL |
| ½ cup | chopped shallots | 125 mL |
| ½ | green pepper, chopped | ½ |
| ½ | red pepper, chopped | ½ |
| 1 to 2 tsp | crushed garlic | 5 to 10 mL |
| 1 tsp | Dhania-jeera Masala (p. 6) or mild curry powder | 5 mL |
| 1 tsp | cornstarch | 5 mL |
| 1 cup | chopped green onions | 250 mL |
| ¾ lb | prepared pasta | 375 g |

1. In small heavy pot, over high heat, bring milk, saffron and bay leaves to just under boiling point, stirring often. When milk turns yellow, remove from heat and set aside.
2. In heavy medium pot, heat oil over high heat. Add shallots and stir-fry for 2 minutes. Add peppers, crushed garlic, dhania-jeera masala and saffron-milk. Bring to just under boiling point.
3. Meanwhile, dissolve cornstarch in a little warm water and add to pot. Reduce heat to low and simmer for 10 minutes. Sauce will be about the consistency of a cream soup. Remove from heat, blend in blender to smooth consistency, add green onions and serve over pasta.

*Serves 4*

## Saffron

Saffron is the world's most expensive spice. Over a quarter of a million crocus flowers yield only a pound of saffron.

The best saffron is grown in Spain, but cheaper Mexican saffron is available as a substitute. You just have to use a lot more. Indians often roast the saffron threads lightly before soaking them in a spoonful of warm water or milk to bring out their golden hue.

**EACH SERVING PROVIDES:**
*(analysis includes pasta)*

| | | |
|---|---|---|
| | Calories | 443 |
| g | Protein | 17 |
| g | Carbohydrates | 81 |
| g | Fibre | 5 |
| g | Fat | 6 |
| g | Saturated Fat | 2 |
| mg | Cholesterol | 9 |
| mg | Sodium | 72 |
| mg | Potassium | 466 |

Excellent: thiamine, riboflavin, vitamin C, iron
Good: niacin, vitamin B-12, vitamin D, folacin, calcium, zinc

# Indian-style Tomato Sauce for Pasta

*This sauce is a variation of the Italian* sugo di pomodoro. *I think the Indian spices make it taste even better. Si!*

*Steamed vegetables or chicken can be added to this sauce for variety.*

| | | |
|---|---|---|
| 2 tbsp | low-fat yogurt | 25 mL |
| ½ cup | cilantro | 125 mL |
| 2 | green chilies, or to taste | 2 |
| 6 | medium fresh roma tomatoes, quartered | 6 |
| 1 tbsp | vegetable oil | 15 mL |
| 1 | medium onion, chopped | 1 |
| 1 tsp | crushed ginger | 5 mL |
| 1 tsp | crushed garlic | 5 mL |
| 2 tsp | Meat Masala (p. 5) | 10 mL |
| ½ tsp | ground turmeric | 2 mL |
| ½ cup | canned crushed tomatoes | 125 mL |
| 1 tsp | salt | 5 mL |
| ¾ lb | prepared pasta | 375 g |

**EACH SERVING PROVIDES:**

*(analysis includes pasta)*

| | | |
|---|---|---|
| | Calories | 428 |
| g | Protein | 14 |
| g | Carbohydrates | 80 |
| g | Fibre | 6 |
| g | Fat | 6 |
| g | Saturated Fat | 1 |
| mg | Cholesterol | trace |
| mg | Sodium | 559 |
| mg | Potassium | 558 |

Excellent: thiamine, vitamin C, iron

Good: riboflavin, niacin, vitamin B-6, folacin, vitamin E, zinc

1. In food processor, blend yogurt, cilantro and green chilies. Add fresh tomatoes and pulse once or twice so tomatoes remain chunky.
2. Heat oil in large pan over medium heat. Add onion and cook until soft. Add ginger, garlic, meat masala and turmeric. Cook for 2 minutes. Add crushed tomatoes, salt and yogurt mixture. Reduce heat to low and cook, stirring, until slightly thickened, about 15 minutes. Longer cooking will only make it better.

*Serves 4*

# Beans & Lentils

꜒ *indicates hot dishes*

# Curried Chickpea Lentils
## CHANNA DAAL

*Daal is the name for split, dried peas, beans and lentils, but also for the dish of spiced lentils, whole or pureed, that accompanies almost every meal. In the cheapest restaurants in India, you buy your bread and the daal is free. The variety of daals is almost infinite, and cooks take great pride in creating something exciting out of the lowly lentil.*

| | | |
|---|---|---|
| 2 cups | lentils, preferably chickpea lentils (channa daal) | 500 mL |
| 6 cups | water | 1.5 L |
| ¾ tsp | crushed ginger | 4 mL |
| ½ tsp | crushed garlic | 2 mL |
| 1 tsp | salt | 5 mL |
| ½ tsp | ground turmeric | 2 mL |
| 1½ tsp | vegetable oil | 7 mL |
| | | |
| 2½ tsp | vegetable oil | 12 mL |
| 2 | cloves | 2 |
| 2-inch | cinnamon stick | 5 cm |
| 1 | cardamom pod | 1 |
| 1 tsp | cumin seeds | 5 mL |
| 1 | medium onion, coarsely chopped | 1 |
| 2 | green chilies (or to taste) halved | 2 |
| 2 | medium tomatoes, cut in big chunks | 2 |
| 1 tbsp | canned crushed tomatoes | 15 mL |
| 1 tsp | Dhania-jeera Masala (p. 6) or mild curry powder | 5 mL |
| ¼ cup | cilantro | 50 mL |
| | lemon juice to taste | |

## EACH SERVING PROVIDES:

*(analysis when served with rice)*

| | | |
|---|---|---|
| | Calories | 462 |
| g | Protein | 21 |
| g | Carbohydrates | 71 |
| g | Fibre | 15 |
| g | Fat | 13 |
| g | Saturated Fat | 1 |
| mg | Cholesterol | 0 |
| mg | Sodium | 858 |
| mg | Potassium | 1182 |

Excellent: thiamine, vitamin B-6, vitamin C, folacin, vitamin E, iron, zinc
Good: riboflavin

1. Rinse lentils, and soak in warm water for 30 to 50 minutes. Drain.
2. In large pot, over high heat, combine 6 cups/1.5 L fresh water, ginger, garlic, salt, ground turmeric and 1½ tsp/7 mL of the oil. Bring to boil and add lentils. When water returns to boil, reduce heat to medium and boil for 20 minutes.
3. Reduce heat to low, cover and simmer until lentils are tender, about 10 minutes. Remove from heat and set aside.

4. Heat remaining oil in small pan over high heat. Add cloves, cinnamon and cardamom pod. When spices start to pop, add cumin seeds and onion. Cook until onion is tender. Add chilies, fresh and crushed tomatoes and dhania-jeera masala. Cook for 2 minutes. Remove from heat and add to lentils.
5. Bring lentil mixture to boil and add cilantro and lemon juice. Serve with rice, or thin it down to a soup with approximately 3 cups/750 mL water. Blend to smooth consistency and serve.

*Serves 4 with rice, 8 to 12 as soup*

| EACH SERVING PROVIDES: | | |
|---|---|---|
| *(analysis when served as soup)* | | |
| | Calories | 154 |
| g | Protein | 7 |
| g | Carbohydrates | 24 |
| g | Fibre | 5 |
| g | Fat | 4 |
| g | Saturated Fat | trace |
| mg | Cholesterol | 0 |
| mg | Sodium | 290 |
| mg | Potassium | 394 |
| Excellent: folacin | | |
| Good: vitamin C, iron | | |

# Mung Bean Lentils
## MOONG DAAL

*The little lentils made from skinned, split mung beans are very quick to prepare, and therefore a favourite with Indian cooks. With mung bean lentils and red lentils, I find that I can start them soaking, put a pot of water on the stove, and by the time the water's boiling, the lentils are ready to be cooked. Moong daal is popular in Northern India.*

| | | |
|---|---|---|
| 2 cups | lentils, preferably dried split mung beans (moong daal) | 500 mL |
| 6 cups | water | 1.5 L |
| 1 tsp | salt | 5 mL |
| ½ | medium onion, chopped | ½ |
| 1 | tomato, cut in large chunks | 1 |
| 1 tsp | ground turmeric | 5 mL |
| 1 tsp | crushed ginger | 5 mL |
| 1 tsp | crushed garlic | 5 mL |
| 1 tsp | minced chilies (to taste) | 5 mL |
| 1 tsp | vegetable oil | 5 mL |
| | | |
| 2 tsp | vegetable oil | 10 mL |
| ½ tsp | mustard seeds | 2 mL |
| ½ tsp | cumin seeds | 2 mL |
| ½ | onion, chopped | ½ |
| 1 | medium tomato, diced | 1 |
| 2 tsp | Dhania-jeera Masala (p. 6) or mild curry powder | 10 mL |
| 2 | green chilies (or to taste), sliced | 2 |
| | chopped cilantro | |
| | lemon juice | |

**EACH SERVING PROVIDES:**

| | | |
|---|---|---|
| | Calories | 316 |
| g | Protein | 19 |
| g | Carbohydrates | 55 |
| g | Fibre | 11 |
| g | Fat | 4 |
| g | Saturated Fat | 1 |
| mg | Cholesterol | 0 |
| mg | Sodium | 729 |
| mg | Potassium | 884 |

Excellent: thiamine, vitamin C, folacin, iron, zinc
Good: vitamin A, vitamin B-6,

1. Rinse lentils, cover with warm water and soak. Bring 6 cups/1.5 L fresh water to boil. Drain lentils and add to boiling water with salt, onion, tomato, turmeric, ginger, garlic, chilies and vegetable oil. Boil, adding more water if needed, until lentils are tender, about 20 minutes. Set aside.
2. Heat oil in small pan over high heat. Add mustard and cumin seeds. When seeds start to pop, add onion and stir-fry until golden brown.

Add tomato, dhania-jeera masala and sliced chilies. Cook for 5 minutes. Remove from heat and add to lentils.

3. Return lentil mixture to stove over high heat, stirring. When mixture comes to boil, immediately remove from heat. Add cilantro and lemon juice before serving.

*Serves 6*

## Turmeric

**Turmeric comes from the dried rhizome of plant that belongs to the ginger family. It's responsible for the bright yellow colour of commercial curry powders and ballpark mustard. The taste is somewhat musky. It is not considered a substitute for saffron.**

# Five Lentils
## PANCHAM DAAL

*Lentil Rules of Thumb*
Soaking helps lentils and
dried beans cook faster
and removes a lot of the
gas-producing com-
pounds. Always discard
the soaking water and
cook in fresh water.
The water should always
be boiling when lentils
go in.
A bit of oil in the cooking
water prevents cooked
lentils from drying out
and becoming crusty.
Lentils are done when
they can be crushed with a
wooden spoon or between
your fingers.

*This recipe is from Karachi, Pakistan, where I had an opportunity to stay
for six months. Our patrons love this so much that we always have it on
the menu. In Indian stores you'll find various lentil combinations. I like
an equal proportion of urad daal, channa daal, red lentils, toor daal and
moong daal, but the supermarket soup mix lentils work well too.*

| | | |
|---|---|---|
| 1 cup | mixed lentils | 250 mL |
| 6 cups | water | 1.5 L |
| 1 tsp | crushed ginger | 5 mL |
| 1 tsp | crushed garlic | 5 mL |
| ½ tsp | ground turmeric | 2 mL |
| 1½ tsp | salt | 7 mL |
| 1 tbsp | vegetable oil | 15 mL |
| | | |
| 1 tbsp | vegetable oil | 15 mL |
| 1 | medium onion, chopped | 1 |
| ½ tsp | cumin seeds | 2 mL |
| 1 | medium tomato, chopped | 1 |
| 1 tsp | Meat Masala (p. 5) | 5 mL |
| | chilies to taste (green or red) | |
| 1 tbsp | cilantro | 15 mL |

1. Wash lentils in hot water and soak for 30 minutes in hot water. Drain.
2. Combine 6 cups/1.5 L fresh water with ginger, garlic, turmeric, salt
   and 1 tbsp/15 mL oil. Bring to boil. Add drained lentils. When water
   returns to boil, turn heat to medium-low. Simmer for 2 hours. Do not
   stir. Mixture will be sticky and smooth.
3. Heat remaining oil in small pan over high heat and saute chopped
   onion and cumin seeds. When onion starts turning light brown, add
   tomato, meat masala and chilies. Stir for 1 minute and mix into lentils.
   If mixture is too thick, add water to thin it down to your liking. Sprinkle with cilantro and serve with boiled rice and pickle of your choice.

*Serves 4*

### EACH SERVING PROVIDES:

| | | |
|---|---|---|
| | Calories | 252 |
| g | Protein | 15 |
| g | Carbohydrates | 33 |
| g | Fibre | 8 |
| g | Fat | 8 |
| g | Saturated Fat | trace |
| mg | Cholesterol | 0 |
| mg | Sodium | 826 |
| mg | Potassium | 604 |

Excellent: folacin, vitamin E,
iron, zinc
Good: vitamin B1, vitamin B-6

See photo, p. 13

# Curried Black Beans
## MAH DI DAAL

*You'll find this dish on the menu every day in Punjab's Sikh temples, where they serve free food. Urad is the word for these small black beans everywhere else in India, but Punjabis call them mah. They develop a creamy texture when cooked. North American black beans are an entirely different variety and can't be used as a substitute.*

| | | |
|---|---|---|
| 1 cup | Indian black beans (urad or mah beans) | 250 mL |
| 6 cups | water | 1.5 L |
| 1 tsp | crushed ginger | 5 mL |
| 1 tsp | crushed garlic | 5 mL |
| 1 tsp | salt | 5 mL |
| ½ tsp | ground turmeric | 2 mL |
| | | |
| 1 tbsp | vegetable oil | 15 mL |
| 1 | medium onion, chopped | 1 |
| 1-inch | piece ginger, grated | 2.5 cm |
| 1 tsp | Sabzi Masala (p. 6) | 5 mL |
| 1 | medium tomato, diced | 1 |
| 2 | green chilies (or to taste), sliced | 2 |
| 2 tbsp | low-fat yogurt | 25 mL |

1. Rinse lentils, cover with water and soak overnight. Drain.
2. Boil 6 cups/1.5 L fresh water, add lentils and boil for 10 to 15 minutes. Skim off foam and reduce heat. Add crushed ginger, garlic, salt and turmeric. Simmer for ½ hour or until beans are tender. Remove from heat and stir vigorously with wooden spoon or eggbeater to break up beans until thick and sticky but still somewhat chunky.
3. Meanwhile, in small skillet, heat oil over medium heat and saute onions and grated ginger until onion is tender. Add sabzi masala, tomato and chilies. Saute for 10 minutes. (This mixture is called *turka* and is often added as a flavour boost to daal.)
4. Whisk yogurt and add to lentils toward end of cooking. Add turka and cook for 2 minutes. If you find the mixture too thick, add some water. Serve with cilantro and lemon on the side so people can garnish as they wish.

*Serves 4*

**EACH SERVING PROVIDES:**

| | | |
|---|---|---|
| | Calories | 231 |
| g | Protein | 13 |
| g | Carbohydrates | 37 |
| g | Fibre | 12 |
| g | Fat | 5 |
| g | Saturated Fat | trace |
| mg | Cholesterol | trace |
| mg | Sodium | 558 |
| mg | Potassium | 675 |

Excellent: folacin, vitamin C, iron

Good: vitamin B1, zinc

# Lentils with Tomato and Onion
## TURKA DAAL

*Turka is a flavour extra for daal. If your daal was prepared the day before, the turka will be added just before serving. It adds a few extra calories, but the flavour makes those extra calories well worth adding.*

| | | |
|---|---|---|
| 1 cup | lentils, preferably half red lentils (masoor daal) and half mung bean lentils (moong daal) | 250 mL |
| 6 to 8 cups | water | 1.5 to 2 L |
| 1 tsp | salt | 5 mL |
| ½ tsp | ground turmeric | 2 mL |
| ½ tsp | crushed ginger | 2 mL |
| ½ tsp | crushed garlic | 2 mL |
| 1 tbsp | vegetable oil | 15 mL |
| | chopped green chilies (optional) | |
| ½ tsp | cumin seeds | 2 mL |
| 2 | cloves garlic, chopped | 2 |
| ½ | medium onion, chopped | ½ |
| 1 | medium tomato, diced | 1 |

1. Rinse lentils, cover with warm water for 20 minutes. Drain.
2. Bring 6 to 8 cups/1.5 to 2 L fresh water to boil. Add lentils, salt, turmeric, crushed ginger and garlic. Boil for 10 minutes. Reduce heat and simmer for 20 minutes or until tender.
3. To prepare turka, heat oil in small skillet over medium heat and saute chilies, cumin, garlic and onion until onion starts browning. Add tomatoes cook for a minute then remove from the heat.
4. Put daal in serving bowl with turka the on top. Serve immediately with lemon juice and cilantro on the side.

*Serves 4*

**EACH SERVING PROVIDES:**

| | | |
|---|---|---|
| | Calories | 209 |
| g | Protein | 14 |
| g | Carbohydrates | 31 |
| g | Fibre | 7 |
| g | Fat | 4 |
| g | Saturated Fat | trace |
| mg | Cholesterol | 0 |
| mg | Sodium | 554 |
| mg | Potassium | 544 |

Excellent: folacin, iron
Good: vitamin B1, vitamin B-6, vitamin E, zinc

# Whole Mung Beans

*What we call mung beans in Canada are known as* moong *beans in India. They're the small green dried beans that are used for bean sprouts.*

*The Gujaratis are very fond of this dish. It goes well with rice and a coleslaw made with raita.*

| | | |
|---|---|---|
| 2 cups | dried mung beans (moong beans) | 500 mL |
| 1 | medium onion | 1 |
| 2 | medium tomatoes | 2 |
| 3 | green chilies, or to taste | 3 |
| 1 tbsp | vegetable oil | 15 mL |
| ½ tsp | mustard seeds | 2 mL |
| ½ tsp | cumin seeds | 2 mL |
| 1 tsp | crushed ginger | 5 mL |
| 1 tsp | crushed garlic | 5 mL |
| 1 tsp | ground turmeric | 5 mL |
| 2 tsp | Sabzi Masala (p. 6) | 10 mL |
| 1 tbsp | canned crushed tomatoes | 15 mL |
| 1 tsp | salt | 5 mL |
| | juice of 1 lemon or 1 cup/250 mL yogurt | |
| 4 to 5 cups | water | 1 to 1.25 L |
| 2 tbsp | chopped cilantro | 25 mL |

1. Cover beans with water and soak overnight. Remove any beans that float. Rinse and drain.
2. Finely chop onion, dice tomatoes and slice chilies.
3. Heat oil in large pot over high heat. Add mustard and cumin seeds. When seeds start to pop, add onion and saute until golden brown.
4. Add ginger, garlic, ground turmeric, sabzi masala, chilies, crushed tomatoes and diced tomatoes. Add mung beans. Mix and bring to boil. Add water, return to boil and cook uncovered until beans are tender and mixture is consistency of porridge, about 15 minutes.
5. Add salt and lemon juice or yogurt (if you use yogurt, whisk smooth before adding). Garnish with cilantro and serve.

*Serves 5*

*Better the Next Day*

**For convenience, the spiced lentil dishes called daals can be made either early in the day or the day before and reheated. The bonus is, they just get better as the flavours meld.**

**You can serve a daal as is the next day or thin it with water and add Sambar Masala (p. 11) for an entirely new dish.**

**EACH SERVING PROVIDES:**

| | | |
|---|---|---|
| | Calories | 389 |
| g | Protein | 23 |
| g | Carbohydrates | 68 |
| g | Fibre | 13 |
| g | Fat | 5 |
| g | Saturated Fat | 1 |
| mg | Cholesterol | 3 |
| mg | Sodium | 450 |
| mg | Potassium | 1119 |

Excellent: thiamine, vitamin C, folacin, iron, zinc
Good: riboflavin, vitamin B-6, vitamin E

# Chickpeas & Potatoes
## AALOO CHOLE

*Chole or chickpeas are very popular in Punjabi cooking. For convenience, this recipe calls for canned chickpeas, but if you prefer to start with dried chickpeas, follow the instructions on the package. When you cook them, the weight and quantity both double. One cup/250 mL of dried chickpeas will make the equivalent of a 14 oz/398 mL tin.*

*This dish is excellent with tamarind chutney and naan bread (p. 109, p. 97) or with mint chutney, chapati and onions (p. 88, p. 100).*

**No More Tears Onions**
If you love onions, you have to cry. But you can cut down the tears a bit; just place onions in the freezer for 5 minutes to cool before you peel and slice them. Don't let them freeze—they'll be useless.

| | | |
|---|---|---|
| 2 | medium potatoes, boiled | 2 |
| 14-ounce | tin chickpeas, rinsed and drained | 398 mL |
| ½ cup | water | 125 mL |
| 1 tbsp | vegetable oil | 15 mL |
| 1 | medium cooking onion, chopped | 1 |
| 1 tsp | crushed ginger | 5 mL |
| 1 tsp | crushed garlic | 5 mL |
| ½ tsp | red chili powder, or to taste | 2 mL |
| ½ tsp | ground turmeric | 2 mL |
| 1 tsp | Sabzi Masala (p. 6) | 5 mL |
| ½ tsp | Garam Masala (p. 6) | 2 mL |
| 1 tsp | salt | 5 mL |
| ½ cup | water | 125 mL |
| 1 | medium mild onion, sliced | 1 |
| 2 tbsp | chopped cilantro | 25 mL |

1. Cut potatoes (peeled or unpeeled) in bite-sized pieces.
2. In large pot over medium heat, combine chickpeas and potatoes. Add water and bring to boil. Remove from heat.
3. In small skillet, heat oil over high heat. Add chopped onion and saute until golden brown. Add ginger, garlic, chili powder, ground turmeric, sabzi masala and garam masala. Cook for 1 minute, then remove from heat.
4. Gently stir onion-spice mixture into potato-bean mixture. Return mixture to stove over high heat. Add salt and ½ cup/125 mL water and bring to boil. Immediately remove from heat. Garnish with sliced onions and cilantro before serving.

**EACH SERVING PROVIDES:**

| | | |
|---|---|---|
| | Calories | 270 |
| g | Protein | 11 |
| g | Carbohydrates | 44 |
| g | Fibre | 8 |
| g | Fat | 7 |
| g | Saturated Fat | 1 |
| mg | Cholesterol | 0 |
| mg | Sodium | 551 |
| mg | Potassium | 733 |

Excellent: folacin, iron
Good: thiamine, vitamin B-6, zinc

*Serves 4*

Chicken Biriani (p. 74)

# Vegetable Dishes

From top: Tamarind Chutney (p. 109), Chicken Tikka (p. 71), Meat and Potato Kebabs (p. 58)

# Balti Vegetables

*This recipe is from Baltistan, a region of Kashmir that borders Afghanistan and China. Feel free to substitute the vegetables of your choice. Add frozen ones toward the end, because they don't need a lot of cooking.*

| | | |
|---|---|---|
| 6 | baby potatoes, whole | 6 |
| ½ cup | broccoli florets | 125 mL |
| ½ cup | cauliflower florets | 125 mL |
| ½ cup | peas | 125 mL |
| ½ cup | corn | 125 mL |
| ½ cup | green beans, cut in 1-inch/2.5 cm pieces | 125 mL |
| 6 | shallots, peeled and halved | 6 |
| ½ | green pepper | ½ |
| ½ | red pepper | ½ |
| 1 tbsp | vegetable oil | 15 mL |
| 1-inch | piece ginger, sliced | 2.5 cm |
| 4 | cloves garlic, crushed | 4 |
| ¼ tsp | crushed carom seeds (optional) | 1 mL |
| ¼ tsp | fennel seeds | 1 mL |
| 1 tsp | cumin seeds | 5 mL |
| 2 tbsp | toasted sesame seeds | 25 mL |
| 1½ tsp | Sabzi Masala (p. 6) | 7 mL |
| ¼ tsp | ground turmeric | 1 mL |
| 6 to 8 | cherry tomatoes | 6 to 8 |
| 1½ tsp | salt | 7 mL |

1. Boil potatoes until done. Blanch broccoli, cauliflower, peas, corn, green beans and shallots separately in rapidly boiling until just becoming tender. Dice peppers.
2. Heat oil in large non-stick pan over high heat. Add shallots, ginger, garlic, carom, fennel, cumin and sesame and saute for 2 minutes or until fragrant. Add sabzi masala and turmeric and cook for 2 more minutes. Add blanched vegetables, cherry tomatoes and salt (do not reduce heat). Toss vegetables to coat with spices. Reduce heat to low and add peppers. Cook covered for 5 minutes.

*Serves 6*

**EACH SERVING PROVIDES:**

| | | |
|---|---|---|
| | Calories | 149 |
| g | Protein | 5 |
| g | Carbohydrates | 28 |
| g | Fibre | 4 |
| g | Fat | 3 |
| g | Saturated Fat | 0 |
| mg | Cholesterol | 0 |
| mg | Sodium | 608 |
| mg | Potassium | 690 |

Excellent: vitamin C

Good: vitamin B-6, folacin, iron

See photo facing p. 84

# Roasted Eggplant
### BENGAN BHARTA

*Eggplant is common to European and Asian cooking. You can easily adapt this recipe to make a Turkish dish known as* baba ganoush. *Just add 1 tbsp/ 15 mL tahini (sesame paste). Although most people in India are familiar with the word* bharta, *different provinces have different names for this dish.*

| | | |
|---|---|---|
| 2 | large eggplants (2 to 3 lb/1 to 1.5 kg total) | 2 |
| 1 tbsp | vegetable oil | 15 mL |
| 1 | medium onion, chopped | 1 |
| 1 tsp | cumin seeds | 5 mL |
| ½-inch | cube ginger, finely chopped | 1 cm |
| 4 | cloves garlic, finely chopped | 4 |
| ¾ tsp | crushed ginger | 4 mL |
| 1 tsp | crushed garlic | 5 mL |
| 2 tsp | Dhania-jeera Masala (p. 6) or mild curry powder | 10 mL |
| 1 tsp | ground turmeric | 5 mL |
| 1 tsp | salt | 5 mL |
| 2 | green chilies (or to taste), crushed | 2 |
| 2 tbsp | canned crushed tomatoes | 25 mL |
| 2 | medium tomatoes, diced | 2 |
| 1 | bunch cilantro, chopped | 1 |
| | juice of 1 lemon | |
| 1 | bunch green onions, finely chopped | 1 |

1. Roast eggplant at 350°F/180°C for 45 minutes. Cool and remove skin, mash eggplant and set aside. (Eggplant can be frozen at this stage for later use.)
2. Heat oil in large pan over high heat. Add onion, cumin, chopped ginger and garlic. Cook until onion is golden brown. Add crushed ginger, crushed garlic, dhania-jeera masala, turmeric, salt, chilies, crushed and diced tomatoes. Cook for 5 minutes until tomatoes are softened. Add mashed eggplant, mix and cook 2 minutes. Remove from heat and add cilantro, lemon juice and green onions before serving.

*Serves 4*

**Eggplant Bengan**
Eggplant is the most widely used vegetable in India. In Canada there are usually two kinds readily available: the large round type and the long seedless Japanese variety. These two varieties have different tastes and textures. The long ones can be cooked and served with little fuss. The larger ones often require salting and draining to remove bitterness before cooking. They can, however, be roasted and peeled, or sliced and barbecued, without salting.

EACH SERVING PROVIDES:
*(analysis as main course)*

| | | |
|---|---|---|
| | Calories | 158 |
| g | Protein | 4 |
| g | Carbohydrates | 27 |
| g | Fibre | 9 |
| g | Fat | 6 |
| g | Saturated Fat | trace |
| mg | Cholesterol | 0 |
| mg | Sodium | 569 |
| mg | Potassium | 938 |

Excellent: vitamin C, folacin
Good: thiamine, vitamin B-6, vitamin E, iron

# Cauliflower & Potatoes

## AALOO GOBI

*Gobi (cauliflower) is a popular vegetable in Punjab. Its flavour works beautifully with Indian spices.*

| | | |
|---|---|---|
| 2 | medium potatoes | 2 |
| 1 | large cauliflower | 1 |
| 2 | medium onions | 2 |
| 1 | medium tomato | 1 |
| 3 | green chilies, or to taste | 3 |
| 4 | cloves garlic | 4 |
| 1-inch | cube ginger | 2.5 cm |
| 1 tbsp | vegetable oil | 15 mL |
| 1 tbsp | canned crushed tomatoes | 15 mL |
| ½ tsp | ground turmeric | 2 mL |
| 1 tsp | Dhania-jeera Masala (p. 6) or mild curry powder | 5 mL |
| 1 tsp | Sabzi Masala (p. 6) | 5 mL |
| 1 tsp | salt | 5 mL |
| ½ cup | chopped green onions | 125 mL |

**EACH SERVING PROVIDES:**

| | | |
|---|---|---|
| | Calories | 160 |
| g | Protein | 5 |
| g | Carbohydrates | 28 |
| g | Fibre | 6 |
| g | Fat | 5 |
| g | Saturated Fat | trace |
| mg | Cholesterol | 0 |
| mg | Sodium | 572 |
| mg | Potassium | 890 |

Excellent: vitamin C, folacin, iron

Good: vitamin B-6, vitamin E

See photo facing p. 13

1. To prepare vegetables, peel potatoes and boil until tender and cut into 1-inch/2.5 cm dice. Cut cauliflower into bite-sized pieces, steam until tender-crisp and set aside.
2. Coarsely chop onions, dice tomato, slice chilies, finely chop garlic and ginger. Set aside.
3. Heat oil in large pan over medium heat. Add chopped onion and saute until tender. Add ginger and garlic and saute for 1 minute. Add crushed tomato, ground turmeric, dhania-jeera masala, sabzi masala, chilies, raw tomato and salt. Cook for 2 minutes and add vegetables. Mix to coat with spices and continue cooking until vegetables are heated through. (Final heating can also be done in microwave in covered dish.) Garnish with green onions and serve with paratha (p. 98) or chapati (p. 100).

*Serves 4*

# Peas & Potatoes
## AALOO MATTER

*This common Gujarati dish has become very popular in North America, maybe because these two vegetables are so familiar here.*

| | | |
|---|---|---|
| 2 | cloves garlic | 2 |
| ½-inch | cube ginger | 1 cm |
| 1 tbsp | vegetable oil | 15 mL |
| ½ tsp | mustard seeds | 2 mL |
| ½ tsp | cumin seeds | 2 mL |
| 2 | large potatoes, boiled | 2 |
| 1 | medium tomato, diced | 1 |
| 1 tsp | ground turmeric | 5 mL |
| 2 tsp | Dhania-jeera Masala (p. 6) or mild curry powder | 10 mL |
| 3 tbsp | canned crushed tomatoes | 45 mL |
| 1 tsp | salt | 5 mL |
| 1 cup | peas (frozen or fresh) | 250 mL |
| 1 cup | water | 250 mL |
| | handful cilantro | |

1. Blend garlic and ginger in blender. Add a little water if necessary.
2. Heat oil over high heat. Add mustard seeds and cumin. When seeds start to pop, add a few pieces of potato to stop spice mixture from burning. Add ginger and garlic paste and cook for 1 minute. Add fresh tomato and cook for 2 minutes. Add ground turmeric, dhania-jeera masala, crushed tomato and salt. Cook for 2 minutes and add peas.
3. When peas are half-cooked, add potatoes and water and bring to boil. Boil for 5 minutes, until thick sauce forms. Remove from heat and add cilantro. Serve immediately. Serve with basmati rice (p. 20) and chapati (p. 100) for a full meal.

*Serves 4*

*Garlic*

Garlic, like onion and ginger, is essential to Indian cooking. Fresh garlic is believed to have many medicinal uses—it's considered a mild antibiotic and also used to protect against the common cold. The bulbs keep well in a dark, dry place. If you prefer to have it peeled and ready to go, keep the peeled cloves in the fridge in a mixture of 1 part vinegar and 3 parts water for up to 5 months. Ginger will also keep this way, but don't keep them together in the same liquid!

**EACH SERVING PROVIDES:**

| | | |
|---|---|---|
| | Calories | 153 |
| g | Protein | 5 |
| g | Carbohydrates | 25 |
| g | Fibre | 5 |
| g | Fat | 5 |
| g | Saturated Fat | trace |
| mg | Cholesterol | 0 |
| mg | Sodium | 579 |
| mg | Potassium | 522 |

Good: thiamine, vitamin B-6, vitamin C, folacin, vitamin E, iron

See photo facing p. 13

# Green Beans & Potatoes

## AALOO VAAL

*The potato is the world's favourite vegetable, and it's no wonder. Is anything more versatile and satisfying? Here it's paired with fresh green beans in a dish that's common all over India.*

| | | |
|---|---|---|
| 1 lb | green beans, stemmed | 500 g |
| ½ lb | potatoes, peeled | 250 g |
| 2 | medium tomatoes | 2 |
| 2 | cloves garlic | 2 |
| ½-inch | cube ginger | 1 cm |
| 1 tsp | vegetable oil | 5 mL |
| ½ tsp | mustard seeds | 2 mL |
| ½ tsp | cumin seeds | 2 mL |
| 1 tsp | salt | 5 mL |
| ½ tsp | ground turmeric | 2 mL |
| ¼ tsp | red chili powder, or to taste | 1 mL |

1. To prepare vegetables, cut uncooked green beans and potatoes into bite-sized pieces and dice tomatoes.
2. Puree ginger and garlic in blender (add a little water if needed).
3. Heat oil in large non-stick pan over high heat. Add mustard seeds and cumin seeds. When seeds start to pop, add diced tomatoes. Cook until tomatoes become soft. Add salt, ground turmeric, chili powder, ginger-garlic mixture, beans and potatoes. Reduce heat to medium and simmer uncovered for 15 minutes or until liquid has cooked away. Serve with chapati (p. 100) or naan (p. 97), or rice.

*Serves 4*

**EACH SERVING PROVIDES:**

| | | |
|---|---|---|
| | Calories | 116 |
| g | Protein | 4 |
| g | Carbohydrates | 24 |
| g | Fibre | 6 |
| g | Fat | 2 |
| g | Saturated Fat | trace |
| mg | Cholesterol | 0 |
| mg | Sodium | 550 |
| mg | Potassium | 618 |

Excellent: vitamin C, folacin
Good: thiamine, vitamin B-6

# Pan-fried Seasoned Okra
## BHINDI

*In England, the Middle East and parts of Africa, these pointed green pods are called ladies' fingers. No matter what the name, it seems this vegetable is known all over the world. No single region of India can claim it as its own.*

| | | |
|---|---|---|
| 2 lb | okra | 1 kg |
| 3 tsp | vegetable oil | 15 mL |
| 2 | medium onions, sliced | 2 |
| 3 tsp | Dhania-jeera Masala (p. 6) or mild curry powder | 15 mL |
| 1 tsp | ground turmeric | 5 mL |
| 1 tsp | red chili powder, or to taste | 5 mL |
| 1 tsp | salt | 5 mL |
| 2 tbsp | canned crushed tomato | 25 mL |
| 1 | tomato, diced | 1 |

1. To prepare vegetables, wipe okra with damp towel (do not rinse or immerse in water) and remove stems. Cut okra lengthwise or into ½-inch/1 cm wheels.
2. Heat 1 tsp/5 mL of the oil over high heat in wok *(karahi)* or skillet. Stir-fry okra until tender in small batches. Add a few drops more oil as necessary. Remove okra from wok and set aside.
3. Heat remaining oil and stir-fry onion. When onion is soft, add dhania-jeera masala, turmeric, chili powder and salt. Stir and cook for 2 minutes. Add crushed tomato and cook for 2 minutes. Add okra and diced tomato and cook for 5 minutes stirring constantly.

*Serves 4*

Okra
Bhindi
**In India, okra is mainly available around monsoon season. In Canada it can usually be found fresh between May and October. Be careful to buy small, firm, light-green okra as the large pods tend to be tough. Frozen and canned okra can be found year-round, and frozen is a particularly good alternative.**

**EACH SERVING PROVIDES:**

| | | |
|---|---|---|
| | Calories | 142 |
| g | Protein | 6 |
| g | Carbohydrates | 25 |
| g | Fibre | 8 |
| g | Fat | 4 |
| g | Saturated Fat | 1 |
| mg | Cholesterol | 0 |
| mg | Sodium | 557 |
| mg | Potassium | 997 |

Excellent: vitamin B-6, vitamin C, folacin
Good: vitamin A, thiamine, vitamin E, calcium, zinc

# Potato-stuffed Crepes
## MASALA DOSA

*If you drew a line through the middle of India separating the North from the South, you'd find the bottom half eating* dosa, *steamed rice bread* (idli) *and thick lentil vegetable soup* (sambar) *for breakfast and lunch. South Indians always eat dosa (they pronounce it "Do say") with coconut chutney.*

*Dosas do take some planning—the rice and lentil mixture for the crepes has to ferment overnight—but fresh dosas with their slightly crisp edges are superb. To save time you can buy commercial mixes for dosas and idli (the basic dough is the same) but the dosas will not be crispy. The spiced potato mixture is the usual stuffing, but feel free to invent and experiment.*

*Crepe (Dosa):*

| | | |
|---|---|---|
| 1½ cups | rice, uncooked | 375 mL |
| ½ cup | Indian black bean lentils (urad daal) | 125 mL |
| 1 tsp | fenugreek seeds (optional) | 5 mL |
| 1 cup | water | 250 mL |
| 1 tsp | salt | 5 mL |
| | vegetable oil spray | |

1. Mix rice, lentils and fenugreek seeds and rinse. Soak in 1 cup water for 2 to 8 hours. Do not drain.
2. In blender or grinder, puree rice-lentil mixture to smooth paste. Cover and let sit in warm place to ferment for 12 hours. Mixture will double in size.
3. Add salt and a little water and stir to consistency of thin pancake batter.
4. Place large non-stick skillet over high heat, spray with vegetable oil and wipe pan to leave just a sheen of oil. Pour in enough batter to thinly cover bottom of pan. It should cook in 3 minutes without flipping.
5. As each dosa is cooked, immediately mound stuffing in centre, fold dosa and serve. Wipe pan again for each dosa.

*Makes 10*

*Potato Stuffing (Masala):*

| | | |
|---|---|---|
| 1 lb | potatoes, peeled | 500 g |
| ¼ cup | vegetable oil | 50 mL |
| 1 tsp | mustard seeds | 5 mL |

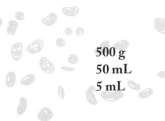

| | | |
|---|---|---|
| 1 tsp | small lentils, preferably Indian | 5 mL |
| | black bean lentils (urad daal) (optional) | |
| | a few curry leaves (optional) | |
| 2 | medium onions cut in long slices | 2 |
| 1 tbsp | minced chilies | 15 mL |
| 1 tsp | crushed ginger | 5 mL |
| 1 tsp | lemon juice | 5 mL |
| | cilantro | |
| 1 tsp | salt | 5 mL |

1. Boil potatoes until tender. Mash half and dice remainder into small cubes.
2. Rinse lentils and drain. Heat small skillet over medium heat and add lentils. Toast until fragrant.
3. Heat oil over high heat. Add mustard seeds. When seeds start to pop, add lentils and curry leaves and cook for 1 minute. Add onions, chilies and ginger. Saute until onions turn soft. Remove from heat and gently fold into mashed and cubed potatoes, lemon juice, cilantro and salt. Set aside. As each dosa is cooked, fill and fold according to illustration. Freshly made dosa always tastes better.

*Serves 8 with stuffing*

# Spicy Corn

*Frozen Corn on the Cob*

**Corn freezes well. Boil cobs until just tender, then cool under running water. Cut into 1-inch/2.5 cm wheels and freeze in self-sealing plastic bags. Reheat in the microwave or steam for a few minutes and you'll bring back memories of late summer.**

*Fresh, sweet corn on the cob is a seasonal treat. Canadians love it with butter and salt, but on the subcontinent there's a more HeartSmart way. You can enjoy this treat year-round if you use frozen corn kernels.*

| | | |
|---|---|---|
| 3 cups | frozen or canned corn kernels or 6 cobs | 750 mL |
| 2 tsp | vegetable oil | 10 mL |
| 1 | medium onion, chopped | 1 |
| 1 | medium tomato, chopped | 1 |
| 1-inch | cube ginger, grated | 2.5 cm |
| 1 tsp | Chili Paste (p. 90) or minced chili | 5 mL |
| ½ cup | water | 125 mL |
| 1 tsp | lemon juice | 5 mL |

1. To prepare fresh corn, put in boiling water and boil covered until kernels are tender. Cut into 1-inch/2.5 cm wheels (don't cut raw corn as this will damage it). For frozen corn, bring corn to boil in a little water and drain immediately. Canned corn need not be precooked.
2. Heat oil over medium heat. Add chopped onion and saute until soft. Mix in tomato, ginger and chili paste. Add water and corn and cook for 3 to 5 minutes, stirring occasionally to ensure corn is evenly coated. Remove from heat, add lemon juice and mix before serving.

*Serves 5*

**EACH SERVING PROVIDES:**

| | | |
|---|---|---|
| | Calories | 105 |
| g | Protein | 3 |
| g | Carbohydrates | 22 |
| g | Fibre | 3 |
| g | Fat | 2 |
| g | Saturated Fat | trace |
| mg | Cholesterol | 0 |
| mg | Sodium | 12 |
| mg | Potassium | 209 |

# Dry-spiced Cauliflower
### SUKHI GOBI

*Cauliflower is considered to be the domain of the Punjabis. They use chickpeas, cauliflower, spinach or fresh cheese in many of their dishes and have given the rest of India some marvelous recipes.*

*In dry curries, the main ingredient is coated with the spices and there is no sauce. This treatment works particularly well for cauliflower.*

*Roll leftover sukhi gobi in a chapati (p. 100), pack up some raita (p. 112) and take it to the office for a deliciously different lunch. Heat it up in the microwave and become the envy of all!*

| | | |
|---|---|---|
| 1 lb | cauliflower | 500 g |
| 1 | clove garlic | 1 |
| 5 | green onions | 5 |
| 1 tbsp | vegetable oil | 15 mL |
| 1 tsp | mustard seeds | 5 mL |
| 1 tsp | salt | 5 mL |
| ½ tsp | ground turmeric | 2 mL |
| 1 tsp | ground almonds | 5 mL |

1. Cut cauliflower into florets. Steam or boil about 4 minutes or until tender-crisp, then drain (do not overcook). Finely chop garlic and cut green onions into ¼-inch/0.5 cm pieces.
2. Heat oil in wok *(karahi)* or skillet over high heat. Add mustard seeds. When they start popping, add garlic, salt and turmeric. Mix and cover. Cook for 2 minutes. Add green onions and ground almonds. Add cauliflower and cook for 3 minutes, stirring constantly, until cauliflower is heated through. Remove from heat and serve as a side dish.

*Serves 6*

**EACH SERVING PROVIDES:**

| | | |
|---|---|---|
| | Calories | 49 |
| g | Protein | 2 |
| g | Carbohydrates | 5 |
| g | Fibre | 2 |
| g | Fat | 3 |
| g | Saturated Fat | trace |
| mg | Cholesterol | 0 |
| mg | Sodium | 380 |
| mg | Potassium | 272 |

Excellent: vitamin C, folacin

# Afro-Indian Spiced Potatoes
## MASALA AALOO

*Masala aaloo is hot and spicy, and it's served with cold, refreshing things. In East African coastal cities and large inland towns, masala aaloo goes with a commercial sparkling drink called Love-O. On the beaches of Dar es Salaam, they serve it with the milk from young coconuts.*

| | | |
|---|---|---|
| 2 lb | potatoes, peeled | 1 kg |
| 1 tbsp | vegetable oil | 15 mL |
| 1 tsp | mustard seeds | 5 mL |
| ½ tsp | cumin seeds | 2 mL |
| 1 tsp | crushed ginger | 5 mL |
| 1 tsp | crushed garlic | 5 mL |
| 1 tsp | Chili Paste (p. 90) or minced chili | 5 mL |
| ½ tsp | ground turmeric | 2 mL |
| 1 tsp | sugar | 5 mL |
| 1 tsp | lemon juice | 5 mL |
| 1 tsp | salt | 5 mL |
| 2 tbsp | canned crushed tomatoes | 25 mL |
| ½ cup | cilantro, chopped | 125 mL |

**EACH SERVING PROVIDES:**

| | | |
|---|---|---|
| | Calories: | 150 |
| g | Protein | 4 |
| g | Carbohydrates | 29 |
| g | Fibre | 3 |
| g | Fat | 3 |
| g | Saturated Fat | trace |
| mg | Cholesterol | 0 |
| mg | Sodium | 370 |
| mg | Potassium | 861 |

Excellent: vitamin C
Good: vitamin B-6

1. Boil potatoes until tender, allow to cool and cut into bite-sized pieces.
2. Heat oil over high heat. Add mustard and cumin seeds. When seeds start to pop, add a few pieces of potato to prevent spices burning. Cook for 2 minutes and add ginger, garlic, chili, ground turmeric, sugar, lemon juice and salt. Cook for 2 minutes and add tomato. Cook for 2 to 3 minutes and add remaining potatoes. Cover and heat potatoes through. Remove from heat and mix well to coat potatoes. Garnish with cilantro and serve.

*Serves 6*

# Fenugreek & Eggplants
## METHI BENGAN

*The nomadic tribespeople of the Indian state of Gujarat eat a variety of dishes at each meal, enjoying small portions from each dish. They often serve methi bengan as either an appetizer, with bread, or a pickle served between dishes. For me, it's a meal with any bread.*

*Try it with spinach instead of fenugreek leaves—a different but also satisfying dish.*

| | | |
|---|---|---|
| 3 bunches | fenugreek leaves | 3 bunches |
| | or 2 bunches spinach, finely chopped | |
| 1 lb | small eggplants | 500 g |
| 1 | medium onion | 1 |
| 2 | cloves garlic | 2 |
| ½-inch | cube ginger | 1 cm |
| 1 | medium tomato | 1 |
| 1 tbsp | vegetable oil | 15 mL |
| 1½ tsp | Dhania-jeera Masala (p. 6) or | 7 mL |
| | mild curry powder | |
| ½ tsp | ground turmeric | 2 mL |
| 1 tsp | Chili Paste (p. 90) or minced chili | 5 mL |

1. Wash and dry fresh fenugreek leaves or spinach. Cut eggplants into bite-sized pieces, slice onion lengthwise, crush garlic and ginger. Dice tomato.
2. Heat oil in wok or large pan over high heat. Add onion and saute until golden brown. Add ginger and garlic. Saute for 2 minutes or until fragrant. Add dhania-jeera masala, turmeric and chili. Cook for 2 minutes. Add tomato, cook uncovered for 3 to 4 minutes or until soft. Add eggplant and mix.
3. Reduce heat to low, cover and cook for 3 minutes until eggplant is tender. Add fenugreek and cook, stirring occasionally, for 5 minutes until very soft. (If using spinach, increase heat to high and cook 1 minute or so longer.)

*Serves 4*

---

*Fenugreek Leaves*
*Methi leaves*
**Fenugreek leaves are a little bitter but very tasty. They are available dried all year long, but fresh leaves appear in Indian and Chinese stores from April to October. The oval, slightly serrated leaves are bright green and grow three to a stem.**

---

**EACH SERVING PROVIDES:**

| | | |
|---|---|---|
| | Calories: | 131 |
| g | Protein | 5 |
| g | Carbohydrates | 20 |
| g | Fibre | 7 |
| g | Fat | 5 |
| g | Saturated Fat | trace |
| mg | Cholesterol | 0 |
| mg | Sodium | 25 |
| mg | Potassium | 522 |

Excellent: iron
Good: folacin, vitamin E

# Indian Cheese
## PANIR

*The Punjabis introduced the subtly flavoured fresh cheese called* panir *to Indian cuisine. It's usually diced in vegetable dishes. In Punjab, panir is often made of high-fat buffalo milk. This panir recipe is made of 1% milk. Firm tofu works as a substitute, but its taste is more bland.*

| | | |
|---|---|---|
| **16 cups** | **1% milk** | **4 L** |
| **2 cups** | **skim-milk powder** | **500 mL** |
| **⅓ cup** | **white vinegar** | **75 mL** |

1. Bring milk and milk powder to boil over high heat. When boiling starts, add vinegar and reduce heat to low. Stir until milk has curdled completely (curds will be solid). Simmer for 30 minutes.
2. Drain in cheesecloth-lined sieve. Flatten into non-stick 13-by-9-inch/ 3 L pan. Cover with clean cheesecloth or J-Cloth and press with rolling pin. Refrigerate for 1 or 2 days. Cut into 1-inch/2.5 cm squares.
3. Before adding panir to dishes, bake for 2 minutes per portion, or microwave for a minute so it will hold its shape.

*Serves 8 (1 oz/30 g or about ⅓ cup/75 mL per serving)*

# Spinach & Indian Cheese
## SAAG PANIR

| | | |
|---|---|---|
| **1 lb** | **spinach** | **500 g** |
| **1 cup** | **broccoli** | **250 mL** |
| **1 tsp** | **vegetable oil** | **5 mL** |
| **1** | **medium onion, diced** | **1** |
| **1 tsp** | **crushed garlic** | **5 mL** |
| **1 tsp** | **crushed ginger** | **5 mL** |
| **2 tsp** | **Sabzi Masala (p. 6)** | **10 mL** |
| **1 tsp** | **minced chilies, or to taste** | **5 mL** |
| **½ tsp** | **salt** | **2 mL** |
| **1 cup** | **Panir (see above) or firm tofu or 2 large potatoes, peeled and diced small** | **250 mL** |

1. In food processor or by hand, finely chop spinach and broccoli.
2. Heat oil in large pan over medium heat. Add onion and saute until transparent. Add garlic, ginger, sabzi masala, chili and salt. Cook for 2 minutes. Add chopped spinach and broccoli. Simmer uncovered for 30 minutes or longer, until all liquid has evaporated and mixture is thick. Add panir. Saute for 10 minutes, until panir is covered with vegetable mixture, and serve.

*Serves 4*

# Peas & Indian Cheese
## MATTER PANIR

| | | |
|---|---|---|
| 1 tbsp | vegetable oil | 15 mL |
| 1 | medium onion, chopped | 1 |
| 2 to 4 | cloves garlic, crushed | 2 to 4 |
| 1-inch | cube ginger, grated | 2.5 cm |
| 2 tsp | Dhania-jeera (p. 6) or mild curry powder | 10 mL |
| 1 tsp | minced chili, or to taste | 5 mL |
| ½ tsp | ground turmeric | 2 mL |
| 1 tsp | salt | 5 mL |
| 2 tbsp | canned crushed tomatoes | 25 mL |
| 1 lb | fresh or frozen peas | 500 g |
| 1 | medium tomato, diced | 1 |
| ½ cup | Panir (see facing page) or firm tofu | 125 mL |
| 1 cup | water | 250 mL |
| 1 tbsp | chopped cilantro | 15 mL |

1. Heat oil in large pan over high heat. Add onion and cook until golden brown. Add garlic and ginger and cook for 2 minutes or until fragrant.
2. Stir in dhania-jeera masala, chili, turmeric, salt, crushed tomato and peas. When peas are half-cooked, add diced tomato. When peas begin to get tender, add water and bring to boil. Reduce heat to low and add panir or tofu and cook for 5 minutes or until peas are done. If not liquid enough, add a little water. Garnish with cilantro and serve.

*Serves 4*

# Mixed Vegetables

*When I was a child, it seemed we had this on our table two hundred days a year. I'm not even sure I really liked it. Still, my mother taught me how to make it and now it's one of my sons' favourite dishes, possibly because I don't serve it as often as Mum did.*

*Use frozen beans if fresh are not available. Just thaw them first.*

| | | |
|---|---|---|
| 1 | medium potato, peeled | 1 |
| 2 | long eggplants (½ lb/250 g total) | 2 |
| 1 | medium tomato | 1 |
| ½ cup | cut romano or other large green beans | 125 mL |
| ½ cup | cut regular green beans | 125 mL |
| ¼ cup | lima beans | 50 mL |
| 2 tsp | vegetable oil | 10 mL |
| ¼ tsp | mustard seeds | 1 mL |
| ¼ tsp | cumin | 1 mL |
| ¼ tsp | ground turmeric | 1 mL |
| 1½ tsp | Dhania-jeera Masala (p. 6) or mild curry powder | 7 mL |
| ¾ tsp | salt | 4 mL |
| ¼ tsp | red chili powder, or to taste | 1 mL |
| 1 tbsp | canned crushed tomatoes | 15 mL |
| ¼ tsp | minced chilies | 1 mL |
| ¼ cup | water | 50 mL |

### EACH SERVING PROVIDES:

| | | |
|---|---|---|
| | Calories | 98 |
| g | Protein | 4 |
| g | Carbohydrates | 17 |
| g | Fibre | 5 |
| g | Fat | 3 |
| g | Saturated Fat | trace |
| mg | Cholesterol | 0 |
| mg | Sodium | 429 |
| mg | Potassium | 490 |

Good: iron

1. Dice potato, cut eggplants into cubes and cut tomato into bite-sized pieces. Thaw beans if frozen.
2. Heat oil in large pot over high heat. Add mustard seeds. When seeds start to pop, add cumin and fresh tomato.
3. Combine turmeric, dhania-jeera masala, salt and chili powder, and add to pot. Cook for 2 minutes. Add all remaining ingredients except eggplant and water. Cook for 5 minutes until potatoes and beans are just becoming tender. Add water if needed and bring to boil. Add eggplant and cook for 5 minutes or until vegetables are tender. Remove from heat and serve.

*Serves 4*

# Indian Roast Potatoes

*Instead of rice, these potatoes are a great accompaniment to any Indian meal, but they'd be a taste sensation in a typical North American meal, next to some simple grilled meat or fish and some steamed vegetables.*

| | | |
|---|---|---|
| 2 tsp | coriander seeds | 10 mL |
| 3 tsp | cumin seeds | 15 mL |
| 2 tsp | red chili flakes, or to taste | 10 mL |
| 1 tbsp | vegetable oil | 15 mL |
| 1 tsp | mustard seeds, preferably black | 5 mL |
| 2 to 3 | cloves garlic, crushed | 2 to 3 |
| 1 tsp | ground turmeric | 5 mL |
| ½ tsp | salt | 2 mL |
| 1½ lb | new baby potatoes, whole | 750 g |

1. Preheat oven to 350°F/180°C.
2. Toast coriander seeds, cumin seeds and chili flakes in unoiled pan over low heat until fragrant. Crush with rolling pin.
3. Heat oil in large pan over high heat. Add mustard seeds. When seeds start to pop, reduce heat to medium and add crushed spice mixture, garlic, turmeric and salt. Cook for 3 minutes. Add potatoes and toss well. Make sure potatoes are evenly coated.
4. Place in unoiled baking pan, cover with foil and bake for 25 minutes or until potatoes are tender. Test for doneness with knife. Serve immediately.

*Serves 5*

*The Life of Spice*

It's always better to buy seeds rather than ground spices. If the recipe calls for ground spices, just use your (well-cleaned) electric coffee grinder or a good mortar and pestle. Whole spices keep their aroma longer and you won't have to buy two versions of the same spice. Keep them in the freezer and they should last a year.

**EACH SERVING PROVIDES:**

| | | |
|---|---|---|
| | Calories | 147 |
| g | Protein | 4 |
| g | Carbohydrates | 27 |
| g | Fibre | 3 |
| g | Fat | 4 |
| g | Saturated Fat | trace |
| mg | Cholesterol | 0 |
| mg | Sodium | 227 |
| mg | Potassium | 799 |

Good: vitamin B-6, vitamin C, iron

# Curried Green Beans
## MASELEDAR VAAL

*Here's an easy green bean dish that fits in perfectly with either an Indian or a Western meal.*

*In Gujarat, where this dish originated, many people don't eat anything that grows under the ground; but in its travels the recipe has picked up some garlic, ginger and turmeric.*

| | | |
|---|---|---|
| 2 lb | french-cut green beans, fresh or frozen | 1 kg |
| 3 | medium tomatoes | 3 |
| 1 tbsp | vegetable oil | 15 mL |
| ½ tsp | mustard seeds | 2 mL |
| ½ tsp | cumin seeds | 2 mL |
| 1 tsp | crushed ginger | 5 mL |
| 1 tsp | crushed garlic | 5 mL |
| 1 tsp | ground turmeric | 5 mL |
| 1 tsp | Sabzi Masala (p. 6) | 5 mL |
| 1 tsp | Dhania-jeera Masala (p. 6) or mild curry powder | 5 mL |
| 1 tbsp | canned crushed tomatoes | 15 mL |
| 1 tsp | salt | 5 mL |
| 1 tsp | minced chili, or to taste | 5 mL |
| 1 cup | water | 250 mL |

1. Cut or slice beans, or thaw if frozen. Dice tomatoes.
2. Heat oil in large pan over high heat. Add mustard and cumin seeds. When seeds start to pop, lower heat to medium and add diced tomatoes, ginger, garlic, turmeric, sabzi masala, dhania-jeera masala, crushed tomato and salt. Cook for 5 minutes, stirring occasionally. Add green beans, chili and water. Simmer until beans are tender, from 5 to 10 minutes depending on thickness of beans. Serve with rice and bread.

*Serves 4*

**EACH SERVING PROVIDES:**

| | | |
|---|---|---|
| | Calories | 150 |
| g | Protein | 6 |
| g | Carbohydrates | 26 |
| g | Fibre | 8 |
| g | Fat | 5 |
| g | Saturated Fat | 1 |
| mg | Cholesterol | 0 |
| mg | Sodium | 565 |
| mg | Potassium | 740 |

Excellent: vitamin C, iron
Good: vitamin A, thiamine, riboflavin, folacin, vitamin E

# Meat Dishes

⟩ *indicates hot dishes*

# Beef Tikka

## Skewer Saver
**Wooden barbecue skewers won't burn up on the grill if you soak them for an hour or so in water before you put the meat on them.**

*This is my sons' favourite midsummer weekend barbecue treat—tikka marinated in their mom's marinade. They bring over fresh summer corn and potatoes and use one of my recipes to cook them. They like to eat it with naan bread (p. 97) and pulao rice (p. 23). Try the combination. I'm sure summer barbecues will never again be the same.*

| | | |
|---|---|---|
| 1½ lb | sirloin tip beef or boneless spring lamb | 750 g |
| 2 tsp | cumin seeds | 10 mL |
| ½ tsp | carom seeds or black pepper | 2 mL |
| 1-inch | piece ginger | 2.5 cm |
| 6 to 8 | cloves garlic | 6 to 8 |
| 2 | red chilies or 1 tsp/5 mL Chili Paste (p. 90), or to taste | 2 |
| 1 tbsp | low-fat yogurt | 15 mL |
| 1 tsp | vegetable oil | 5 mL |

1. Cut meat into 1 inch/2.5 cm cubes and set aside.
2. Toast cumin and carom seeds over low heat in small heavy unoiled pan. Remove from heat when fragrant. (Not necessary for black pepper.)
3. In blender, blend seeds and remaining ingredients into paste. Stir in meat until coated with marinade and marinate in refrigerator for 6 to 8 hours.
4. Thread on skewers and barbecue, turning, for 10 minutes. Serve with raita, tamarind or mint chutney (p. 112, p. 109, p. 88) and one of the cachumbar relishes (p. 18).

*Serves 4*

## EACH SERVING PROVIDES:

*(analysis includes raita and tamarind chutney)*

| | | |
|---|---|---|
| | Calories | 321 |
| g | Protein | 42 |
| g | Carbohydrates | 10 |
| g | Fibre | 1 |
| g | Fat | 12 |
| g | Saturated Fat | 4 |
| mg | Cholesterol | 117 |
| mg | Sodium | 336 |
| mg | Potassium | 724 |

Excellent: vitamin A, riboflavin, niacin, vitamin B-12, vitamin B-6, vitamin C, iron, zinc
Good: thiamine

# Indian Burgers
## KATI KEBAB

*The Moguls introduced kebabs, and they're still very popular around Delhi, which was the capital of the Mogul Empire. The Moguls came from Iran and the word* kebab *is found not only in the Middle Eastern dialects, but in parts of Europe, such as Greece and Romania.*

| | | |
|---|---|---|
| 1 | slice stale white bread | 1 |
| ¼ tsp | crushed ginger | 1 mL |
| ¼ tsp | crushed garlic | 1 mL |
| ¼ tsp | Meat Masala (p. 5) | 1 mL |
| 1 tsp | minced green chilies, or to taste | 5 mL |
| ¼ tsp | salt | 1 mL |
| 1 tsp | finely chopped onions | 5 mL |
| 1 tsp | chopped cilantro | 5 mL |
| ½ lb | ground lamb | 250 g |
| | whole wheat flour for dusting | |

1. Crush bread to fine crumbs. (If bread is too soft, bake on low temperature until dry.)
2. In large mixing bowl, combine all ingredients except meat. Mix well, then add meat. Mix well, then divide mixture into 4 equal balls. Flatten into patties and dust with whole wheat flour.
3. Wrap and freeze unused portions immediately. (Separate patties with waxed paper.)
4. To serve as hamburgers, fry in non-stick pan over high heat until browned on both sides. Or, to make appetizer-sized kebabs, divide meat mixture into 8 portions, wrap them around skewers and barbecue.

*Serves 4 with bun and salad*

## Ground Meats
**When purchasing ground beef you can make sure it's lean or extra-lean by reading the label. With other meats, to cut down the total amount of fat and saturated fat, your best bet is to buy a lean cut and grind it yourself in a meat grinder or food processor.**

**EACH SERVING PROVIDES:**
*(analysis without bun or salad)*

| | | |
|---|---|---|
| | Calories | 136 |
| g | Protein | 11 |
| g | Carbohydrates | 5 |
| g | Fibre | 1 |
| g | Fat | 8 |
| g | Saturated Fat | 3 |
| mg | Cholesterol | 38 |
| mg | Sodium | 202 |
| mg | Potassium | 194 |

Excellent: vitamin B-12
Good: zinc

# Meat & Potato Kebabs

*My diet is almost entirely vegetarian. My husband and sons were the exact opposite, and I thought I should try to get them to reduce their meat intake. They love kebabs, so that's where I started. I reduced the meat in this recipe and they liked it. This nice light lunch was the beginning of a fresh approach to their meals.*

| | | |
|---|---|---|
| 2 lb | potatoes, peeled | 1 kg |
| 1 lb | extra-lean ground beef or lamb | 500 g |
| ½ tsp | salt | 2 mL |
| 1 tsp | Meat Masala (p. 5) | 5 mL |
| 1 tsp | crushed ginger | 5 mL |
| 1 tsp | crushed garlic | 5 mL |
| ½ tsp | ground cumin | 2 mL |
| ¼ tsp | Garam Masala (p. 6) | 1 mL |
| 1 | medium onion, finely chopped | 1 |
| ½ cup | chopped cilantro | 125 mL |
| 1 cup | dry breadcrumbs | 250 mL |
| 3 | eggs | 3 |

**EACH SERVING PROVIDES:**

*(analysis with lamb)*

| | | |
|---|---|---|
| | Calories | 168 |
| g | Protein | 12 |
| g | Carbohydrates | 22 |
| g | Fibre | 2 |
| g | Fat | 4 |
| g | Saturated Fat | 1 |
| mg | Cholesterol | 64 |
| mg | Sodium | 196 |
| mg | Potassium | 557 |

Excellent: vitamin B-12
Good: vitamin B-6, iron, zinc

See photo, p. 37

1. Boil potatoes until tender and mash. (Do not add butter or milk.)
2. In large non-stick pan, combine meat with salt, meat masala, ginger, garlic and cumin over medium heat. Cook until meat juices have evaporated. Cool meat in strainer.
3. In bowl, mix garam masala, onion and cilantro with cooled meat.
4. Mix meat and mashed potatoes. To make kebabs, roll into sausage shapes about 2 inches/5 cm long. Pour breadcrumbs onto sheet of waxed paper. Beat eggs. Dip kebabs into eggs and roll in breadcrumbs.
5. Broil under 400°F/200°C broiler or in 350°F/180°C toaster oven (top and bottom elements) until golden brown.

*Serves 12 (as appetizer)*

# Beef Gobi

Gobi *means "cauliflower" or "cabbage." Shakilabanu, the excellent cook who introduced me to this dish, told me this way of cooking it was very popular in Lahore, Pakistan. It's become very popular in my house too.*

*Beef and Marinade:*

| | | |
|---|---|---|
| ½ tsp | salt | 2 mL |
| 1 tsp | crushed ginger | 5 mL |
| 1 tsp | crushed garlic | 5 mL |
| 1 lb | aged tender stewing beef, cubed | 500 g |
| | | |
| 1 tbsp | vegetable oil | 15 mL |
| 1 | medium onion sliced | 1 |
| 1 tsp | Meat Masala (p. 5) | 5 mL |
| 1 tsp | Sabzi Masala (p. 6) | 5 mL |
| ½ tsp | ground turmeric | 2 mL |
| 1 tbsp | canned crushed tomatoes | 15 mL |
| 1 lb | cauliflower in small florets | 500 g |
| ½ tsp | salt | 2 mL |

1. To prepare marinade, combine salt, ginger and garlic. Toss beef with marinade to coat. Cover and marinate in fridge for 2 hours or overnight.
2. Heat oil in large pan over high heat. Add onion and cook until tender. Stir in meat masala, sabzi masala, turmeric and tomato. Add beef, and cook until browned.
3. Reduce heat to low and cook for 10 to 15 minutes until mixture is thick but not dry. Increase heat to high, add cauliflower and salt and cook for 10 minutes until cauliflower is tender.

*Serves 4*

**EACH SERVING PROVIDES:**

| | | |
|---|---|---|
| | Calories | 244 |
| g | Protein | 24 |
| g | Carbohydrates | 11 |
| g | Fibre | 4 |
| g | Fat | 12 |
| g | Saturated Fat | 3 |
| mg | Cholesterol | 70 |
| mg | Sodium | 764 |
| mg | Potassium | 584 |

Excellent: vitamin B-12, vitamin C, vitamin C, folacin, vitamin E, iron, zinc
Good: riboflavin, vitamin B-6

# Cassava with Meat

Cassava
Manioc root, yuca
**Cassava, a root vegetable native to Latin America, was taken to East Africa by the Portuguese. It's available in Asian or specialty grocery stores fresh, frozen, dried or fermented. Like the potato, cassava is high in carbohydrates, and potatoes can stand in as a substitute in some recipes. Cassava is the source of tapioca.**

*In our restaurant in London, this was our most requested recipe. It has its roots in the East African dish* mhogo na nyama, *which was adopted as a staple by the Indians who moved there. The Indians added their own touches.*

*In some recipes you can replace cassava with potatoes, but that won't work in this one—the texture just isn't right. Look for fresh or frozen cassava in Asian or Latin American stores.*

| | | |
|---|---|---|
| 1 lb | fresh or frozen cassava | 500 g |
| ½ lb | boneless beef or poultry | 250 g |
| 2 | green chilies, or to taste | 2 |
| 1 | medium tomato | 1 |
| 6 cups | water | 1.5 L |
| 1 tsp | salt | 5 mL |
| 1 tsp | crushed ginger | 5 mL |
| 1 tsp | crushed garlic | 5 mL |
| 1 cup | low-fat yogurt | 250 mL |
| 1 tbsp | chopped cilantro | 15 mL |

1. Cut cassava into 1-inch/2.5 cm cubes; cut meat into cubes half that size. Slice chilies and dice tomato.
2. Bring water to boil over high heat. Add cassava and meat, chilies, salt, ginger and garlic. Reduce heat and simmer until meat is half-cooked. Add tomato and cook until meat is very tender. Mix in yogurt and remove from heat. Garnish with cilantro and serve with coconut chutney (p. 108) or tamarind chutney (p. 109).

*Serves 4*

**EACH SERVING PROVIDES:**

| | | |
|---|---|---|
| | Calories | 266 |
| g | Protein | 20 |
| g | Carbohydrates | 36 |
| g | Fibre | 2 |
| g | Fat | 5 |
| g | Saturated Fat | 2 |
| mg | Cholesterol | 42 |
| mg | Sodium | 632 |
| mg | Potassium | 1244 |

Excellent: riboflavin, vitamin B-12, vitamin B-6, vitamin C, iron, zinc
Good: thiamine B1, niacin, folacin, calcium

# Beef Curry

*Beef is eaten mostly in Pakistan. In India, the majority Hindus respect the cow because it gives milk, and it is considered a sacred animal. The Christians in the South and the Muslims who live in predominantly Muslim areas eat it, though. This mouthwatering dish originated with the Muslims.*

| | | |
|---|---|---|
| 1 tbsp | vegetable oil | 15 mL |
| 2-inch | cinnamon stick | 5 cm |
| 4 | cloves | 4 |
| 4 | cardamom pods | 4 |
| 2 | medium onions, sliced | 2 |
| 1 tsp | crushed garlic | 5 mL |
| 1 tsp | crushed ginger | 5 mL |
| 1 lb | cubed lean stewing beef | 500 g |
| ¼ cup | low-fat yogurt | 50 mL |
| 1 tsp | salt | 5 mL |
| 1 tsp | Meat Masala (p. 5) | 5 mL |
| 1 | green chili (or to taste), sliced | 1 |
| 1 | medium tomato, cut in quarters | 1 |
| 1 cup | water | 250 mL |
| 2 | medium potatoes, boiled, cut in 8 pieces each | 2 |
| 2 tbsp | chopped cilantro | 25 mL |

1. Heat oil; add cinnamon, cloves and cardamom. When seeds start popping, add onions and stir-fry until golden brown. Cook for 2 minutes and add all other ingredients except boiled potatoes and cilantro. Cook covered until meat is tender. Cooking time will vary from 25 to 40 minutes.
2. When meat is tender, add potatoes and bring to boil so potatoes can absorb flavours. Add water if sauce is too thick. Remove cinnamon stick, sprinkle with cilantro and serve.

*Serves 4*

**EACH SERVING PROVIDES:**

| | | |
|---|---|---|
| | Calories | 284 |
| g | Protein | 25 |
| g | Carbohydrates | 19 |
| g | Fibre | 3 |
| g | Fat | 12 |
| g | Saturated Fat | 4 |
| mg | Cholesterol | 71 |
| mg | Sodium | 763 |
| mg | Potassium | 740 |

Excellent: vitamin B-12, iron, zinc

Good: riboflavin, vitamin B-6, vitamin C, vitamin E

See photo facing p. 84

# Beef Vindaloo

**EACH SERVING PROVIDES:**

|  |  |  |
|---|---|---|
|  | Calories | 254 |
| g | Protein | 29 |
| g | Carbohydrates | 15 |
| g | Fibre | 3 |
| g | Fat | 9 |
| g | Saturated Fat | 3 |
| mg | Cholesterol | 77 |
| mg | Sodium | 655 |
| mg | Potassium | 805 |

Excellent: vitamin B-12,
vitamin B-6, iron, zinc
Good: thiamine, riboflavin,
niacin, vitamin C

*For many years now, a loyal customer of ours has taken home beef
vindaloo every Friday or Saturday night. When his wife is away,
every night becomes a Friday or Saturday night!*

*This fiery dish was introduced by the Portuguese and perfected
by the Goans. Have some raita on hand to cool yourself down.*

*Meat and Marinade:*

| | | |
|---|---|---|
| ½ tsp | crushed ginger | 2 mL |
| ½ tsp | crushed garlic | 2 mL |
| ½ tsp | salt | 2 mL |
| 1 lb | cubed boneless lean stewing beef or pork, or on-the-bones stewing goat | 500 g |
| 1 tsp | vegetable oil | 5 mL |
| 1-inch | cinnamon stick | 2.5 cm |
| 4 | cloves | 4 |
| 2 | cardamom pods | 2 |
| ½ tsp | crushed ginger | 2 mL |
| ½ tsp | crushed garlic | 2 mL |
| 1 | medium onion, finely chopped | 1 |
| 4 | dried chilies | 4 |
| ½ tsp | salt | 2 mL |
| 2 tsp | Meat Masala (p. 5) | 10 mL |
| ¼ tsp | ground turmeric | 1 mL |
| 2 tsp | brown sugar | 10 mL |
| 2 tbsp | wine vinegar | 25 mL |
| 2 | medium tomatoes, diced | 2 |
| 1 cup | water | 250 mL |
| 1 tbsp | tomato paste | 15 mL |
| | vegetable oil spray | |
| 1 | large potato, quartered | 1 |

1. To prepare marinade, mix crushed ginger, crushed garlic and salt.
   Combine meat with marinade and marinate in fridge for 20 minutes
   or overnight.

2. Heat oil over medium heat. Add cinnamon, cloves and cardamom and cook until fragrant. Stir in ginger and garlic. Add onion and saute until golden brown. Reduce heat to low, add remaining spices, brown sugar, wine vinegar and tomatoes. Bring to boil and cook for 2 minutes. Remove from heat.
3. Remove cinnamon stick. Puree remaining mixture in blender.
4. Lightly coat pan with vegetable oil spray and place over medium heat. Add marinated meat and saute until browned. Add sauce from blender and saute for 15 minutes. Add potato, reduce heat, cover and simmer until meat and potato are tender. Remove from heat and serve with rice or as a side dish.

*Serves 4*

*Fresh Ginger*

**Whole ginger root may become dry after it sits too long. To revitalise dry ginger, soak in warm water (if it's mouldy, don't bother). To keep ginger fresh without compromising too much flavour, store it whole in the freezer or keep it immersed in 1 part vinegar and 3 parts water in the fridge. It will keep for about 5 months.**

# Lamb Pulao

*This simple dish is called* pilaf *in the Middle East where it originated. In the Indian community it's been adopted enthusiastically.*

*In my family, it wasn't Sunday if there was no pulao. In East Africa we added goat meat, but in England we used mutton since it was the closest thing to goat meat that was readily available. My elder son still keeps this tradition. Sunday is still goat pulao day in his family.*

| | | |
|---|---|---|
| 2 cups | basmati or other long-grain rice | 500 mL |
| 6 to 8 | cloves garlic | 6 to 8 |
| 1-inch | piece ginger, sliced | 2.5 cm |
| 5 cups | water | 1.25 L |
| 1 lb | lean lamb, cut in ¾-inch/2 cm cubes | 500 g |
| 1½ tsp | salt | 7 mL |
| 2 tbsp | vegetable oil | 25 mL |
| 1 | cinnamon stick | 1 |
| 2 | cloves | 2 |
| 4 | cardamom pods | 4 |
| 1 tsp | cumin seeds | 5 mL |
| 1 | small onion, sliced | 1 |
| 5 | peppercorns | 5 |
| 1 | medium tomato, diced | 1 |
| | juice of ½ lemon | |
| 1 | green chili (or to taste), sliced | 1 |
| 1 | large potato, cut in large chunks | 1 |

1. Rinse rice well and soak in warm water for 20 minutes.
2. In blender, puree ginger and garlic with a little water to smooth paste.
3. Bring water to boil. Add lamb, ½ tsp/2 mL of the salt and half the ginger/garlic mixture. Reduce heat and simmer lamb for 15 minutes or until tender. Strain cooking liquid into bowl and set meat aside.
4. Place large ovenproof pot over high heat and heat oil. Add cinnamon, cloves and cardamom. When spices start to pop, add cumin seeds, sliced onion and peppercorns. Saute until onion is transparent (do not brown). Add remaining ginger/garlic blend, diced tomato, lemon juice, sliced chili and potatoes. Add cooking liquid and remaining 1 tsp/5 mL

salt (if there is less then 4 cups cooking liquid, top it up with water) and bring to boil.

5. Preheat oven to 350°F/180°C.
6. Drain rice and add to pot. Cook for 10 minutes and gently fold in lamb.
7. Remove from heat, cover and place in oven. Bake for 20 minutes.

*Serves 4*

**EACH SERVING PROVIDES:**

|    | Calories | 643 |
|----|----------|-----|
| g  | Protein | 33 |
| g  | Carbohydrates | 95 |
| g  | Fibre | 3 |
| g  | Fat | 15 |
| g  | Saturated Fat | 3 |
| mg | Cholesterol | 73 |
| mg | Sodium | 873 |
| mg | Potassium | 645 |

Excellent: niacin, vitamin B-12, vitamin C, vitamin E, zinc
Good: riboflavin, Vitmain B-6, folacin, iron

# Traditional Lamb Curry

*I was born to a vegetarian family and had never touched meat until I
married. The first dinner I attended after my marriage included only one
vegetarian dish, so I knew I had to learn fast. This was the first dish my
husband taught me. Here is simple one-step cooking at its tastiest.*

| | | |
|---|---|---|
| 2-to-3-lb | **leg of lamb, bone-in** | 1 to 1.5 kg |
| ½ cup | **low-fat yogurt** | 125 mL |
| 1½ tsp | **salt** | 7 mL |
| 1 tsp | **crushed ginger** | 5 mL |
| 1 tbsp | **crushed garlic** | 15 mL |
| 2 | **medium onions sliced** | 2 |
| 1 tsp | **Meat Masala (p. 5)** | 5 mL |
| 1 | **green chili, or to taste** | 1 |
| 1 tbsp | **tomato paste** | 15 mL |
| 2 cups | **water** | 500 mL |
| 2-inch | **cinnamon stick** | 5 cm |
| 4 | **cloves** | 4 |
| ⅛ | **star anise (1 petal)** | ⅛ |
| 2 | **medium boiled potatoes, cut in 8 pieces** | 2 |
| | **(uncooked if using pressure cooker)** | |
| 2 tbsp | **chopped cilantro** | 25 mL |

1. To prepare lamb, remove all visible fat and cut into stewing pieces.
   Reserve bones. Yield will be less than 2 lb/1kg meat.
2. Combine meat and bones with next 9 ingredients down to water.
3. Heat large heavy unoiled pan (or pressure cooker) over low heat.
   Toast cinnamon, cloves and star anise until fragrant.
4. Regular method: Add meat mixture to spices. Increase heat to medium
   and simmer covered for about 30 minutes or until meat becomes tender.
   Add boiled potatoes. Bring to boil to heat potatoes.
   Pressure cooker method: Add meat mixture and raw potatoes. Cook
   in pressure cooker for 15 minutes. Remove from stove and wait until
   pressure is gone.
5. Remove bones. Garnish dish with cilantro before serving.

*Serves 6*

# Poultry Dishes

❱ *indicates hot dishes*

# Cocktail Samosas

*These delicious turnovers are usually deep-fried, but I did some experimenting and came up with this version, in response to requests from patrons.*

*They are fairly labour-intensive, but they freeze beautifully. You can make them when you have time, then, when your guests are about to arrive, pop them in the oven without even thawing. The pastry also freezes well.*

*Filling:*

| | | |
|---|---|---|
| | vegetable oil spray | |
| ¾ lb | skinless, boneless chicken breasts, cut in small chunks | 375 g |
| ½ | regular onion, sliced | ½ |
| 1½ tsp | crushed ginger | 7 mL |
| 1½ tsp | crushed garlic | 7 mL |
| ½ tsp | salt | 2 mL |
| 1½ tsp | Meat Masala (p. 5) | 7 mL |
| ½ tsp | ground cumin | 2 mL |
| ½ tsp | Chili Paste (p. 90) or minced chilies to taste | 2 mL |
| ¼ tsp | Garam Masala (p. 6) | 1 mL |
| 2 bunches | green onions, finely chopped | 2 bunches |
| ¼ cup | coarsely chopped cilantro | 50 mL |

1. Spray non-stick skillet with vegetable oil and heat over medium heat. Add other ingredients down to chili paste and stir-fry until all juices have disappeared. Remove from heat and let cool completely.
2. Mince mixture to consistency of ground meat. Stir in garam masala, green onions and cilantro.

*Pastry:*

| | | |
|---|---|---|
| ½ tsp | salt | 2 mL |
| 2 cups | all-purpose flour | 500 mL |
| 5 tsp | lime or lemon juice | 25 mL |
| ¾ cup | lukewarm water | 175 mL |
| 4 tbsp | vegetable oil | 60 mL |
| | dusting flour | |
| | vegetable oil spray | |

| ½ cup | water | 125 mL |
|---|---|---|
| 2 tbsp | flour | 25 mL |

1. Stir together salt and flour. Work lime juice and water into flour with hands to form stiff dough. Knead until dough is still sticky but no longer adheres to sides of bowl (add a few drops more water if dough is too dry). Leave in warm place for at least 10 minutes.
2. Knead again for 1 minute and roll by hand into 1½-foot/45 cm roll. Divide into 12 equal balls.
3. With rolling pin, flatten 1 ball into 5-inch/12 cm round. Brush top with oil. Sprinkle with flour and smooth out flour by hand. Roll out next ball to same size. Brush both sides with oil, stack on top of first round, dust top with flour. Repeat to make stack of 4 rounds. Make 3 stacks of 4 rounds each. With rolling pin, roll each stack to 10-inch/25 cm round.
4. Lightly oil large skillet and heat over medium heat. Place 1 stack in pan and cook for 45 seconds. Flip stack, separate and remove top layer with tongs or hands. (Cooked pastry will have developed bubbles and will still be very flexible.). Continue flipping and removing top layer until all layers are cooked. Repeat for each stack. (Pastry may be frozen for later use at this stage.)
5. Cut each round into 3 strips. Fold into cone according to diagram and fill with approximately 1 tsp/5 mL filling. Continue folding until filling is completely enclosed.
6. Mash together flour and water to make paste. Spread paste inside exposed flaps of pastry and press to seal. Press corners to seal. (Samosas may be frozen at this stage—freeze on cookie sheet, then put in freezer bags.)
7. Preheat broiler or toaster oven (top and bottom elements) to 500°F/260°C. Spray samosas on both sides with vegetable oil spray and place on cookie sheets. Broil approximately 5 minutes, turning once, or until pastry is golden. Serve with tamarind chutney (p. 109) or mint chutney (p. 88).

*Makes 36, serves 18*

**EACH SERVING PROVIDES:**

*(analysis with chicken filling)*

| | Calories | 106 |
|---|---|---|
| g | Protein | 6 |
| g | Carbohydrates | 12 |
| g | Fibre | 1 |
| g | Fat | 4 |
| g | Saturated Fat | trace |
| mg | Cholesterol | 10 |
| mg | Sodium | 130 |
| mg | Potassium | 74 |

# Indian Chicken Burgers
## CHAPLI KEBAB

*This dish is traditionally made with ground beef. My granddaughter prefers chicken in this dish and who am I to argue. I find chicken tenders, the narrow filets attached to the breast meat, make for particularly juicy kebabs.*

| | | |
|---|---|---|
| 2 lb | chicken tenders or skinless, boneless chicken breast | 1 kg |
| ½ | medium onion | ½ |
| 2 | slices day-old bread | 2 |
| ½ cup | green onions | 125 mL |
| ¼ cup | cilantro | 50 mL |
| 1 | egg | 1 |
| 1 tsp | Meat Masala (p. 5) | 5 mL |
| 1 tsp | salt | 5 mL |
| 3 | green chilies, or to taste | 3 |
| 1 tsp | vegetable oil | 5 mL |

1. Chop chicken to hamburger consistency. (Ground chicken from supermarket will eliminate this step, but will have higher fat content.)
2. In food processor, combine all ingredients except chicken by pulsing a few times.
3. Combine food processor mixture with chicken and mix well. Divide into 6 equal balls. Wet hands and flatten balls into patties.
4. Brush griddle, skillet or barbecue grill with oil or lightly coat with vegetable oil spray before cooking. Cook on both sides over high heat until patties are firm and opaque.
5. Serve on bun and use all or any of the following: lettuce, tomato, cucumber, tamarind chutney, raita or any low-fat relish in moderation.

*Serves 6*

**EACH SERVING PROVIDES:**

| | | |
|---|---|---|
| | Calories | 236 |
| g | Protein | 37 |
| g | Carbohydrates | 10 |
| g | Fibre | 1 |
| g | Fat | 5 |
| g | Saturated Fat | 1 |
| mg | Cholesterol | 121 |
| mg | Sodium | 496 |
| mg | Potassium | 377 |

Excellent: niacin, vitamin C
Good: riboflavin, vitamin B-12, vitamin B-6, iron, zinc

# Chicken Tikka

Tikka *simply means "cut in bite-sized chunks." It tastes great any which way you cook it, but for best flavour use a tandoor oven or barbecue. You can roll the tikka in a naan (p. 97) or other flatbread with a salad of your choice and use raita and tamarind sauce (p. 112, p. 109) for dressing.*

| 1 lb | skinless, boneless chicken breast | 500 g |
|------|-----------------------------------|-------|
| 1 tsp | crushed ginger | 5 mL |
| 1 tsp | crushed garlic | 5 mL |
| 1 tsp | ground cumin | 5 mL |
| ¼ tsp | red chili powder, or to taste | 1 mL |
| ¼ tsp | Chili Paste (p. 90) or minced chili (optional) | 1 mL |
| ¼ cup | low-fat yogurt | 50 mL |
| 2 tsp | vegetable oil | 10 mL |
| ¾ tsp | salt | 4 mL |
| | 2 to 3 drops red & yellow food colouring (optional) | |

1. Cut chicken into ¾-inch/2 cm cubes. Stir together remaining ingredients to make marinade. Stir in chicken to coat and marinate for 2 hours or more in refrigerator.
2. Preheat oven to 400°F/200°C or start barbecue.
3. Thread chicken onto skewers. For best results, barbecue on both sides until opaque and firm to the touch. Or, bake for 6 minutes on broiling pan or cake rack over baking pan (so any fat drains away). Serve with tamarind chutney and coleslaw made with raita.

*Serves 6 as appetizer*

**EACH SERVING PROVIDES:**

| | | |
|---|---|---|
| | Calories | 118 |
| g | Protein | 18 |
| g | Carbohydrates | 1 |
| g | Fibre | trace |
| g | Fat | 4 |
| g | Saturated Fat | 1 |
| mg | Cholesterol | 45 |
| mg | Sodium | 324 |
| mg | Potassium | 142 |
| Good: niacin | | |

See photo facing p. 37

# Chicken Breast with Vegetables
## SABZI-MURG

*Reserve a place for this quick, simple recipe on your summer menu, because it's especially delicious with whole baby carrots and potatoes.*

| | | |
|---|---|---|
| ½ tsp | carom seeds or dill seeds | 2 mL |
| ½ tsp | cumin seeds | 2 mL |
| 1 tsp | Chili Paste (p. 90) or red chili powder | 5 mL |
| ½ | red pepper | ½ |
| 4 | cloves garlic | 4 |
| 1 tbsp | tomato paste | 15 mL |
| 2 tbsp | low-fat yogurt | 25 mL |
| ½-inch | piece ginger | 1 cm |
| 1 tbsp | vegetable oil | 15 mL |
| 1 | medium onion, sliced | 1 |
| 8 | baby potatoes, whole | 8 |
| 8 | baby carrots, whole | 8 |
| 6 | shallots, peeled | 6 |
| 1 tsp | salt | 5 mL |
| ¾ lb | skinless chicken parts | 375 g |
| 1 tsp | chopped fenugreek leaves or parsley | 5 mL |
| 1 tsp | toasted sesame seeds | 5 mL |

**EACH SERVING PROVIDES:**

| | | |
|---|---|---|
| | Calories | 267 |
| g | Protein | 24 |
| g | Carbohydrates | 34 |
| g | Fibre | 4 |
| g | Fat | 4 |
| g | Saturated Fat | 1 |
| mg | Cholesterol | 51 |
| mg | Sodium | 638 |
| mg | Potassium | 821 |

Excellent: niacin, vitamin B-6, vitamin C
Good: Thamine, folacin, iron

1. Preheat oven to 350°F/180°C.
2. Toast carom and cumin seeds in unoiled pan over low heat until fragrant. Remove from heat and crush coarsely.
3. Puree chili paste, red pepper, garlic, tomato paste, yogurt and ginger in food processor and set aside.
4. Heat oil in large pan over medium heat. Add onion and cook until tender. Add potatoes, carrots and shallots to pan and cook for 5 minutes. Add food processor mixture, toasted spices and salt. Increase heat to high, bring to boil, then remove from heat.
5. Spread chicken in ovenproof dish and evenly spread vegetable mixture over top. Bake covered for about 20 to 30 minutes. When done, sprinkle with fenugreek leaves and sesame seeds. Broil for 5 minutes and serve.

*Serves 4*

# Roast Quail
## BATER

*Traditionally, travellers hunted quail and partridge in the mountainous areas of Northern India. Quail is considered a delicacy, but is available in supermarkets in Canadian cities. Most quail available in Canada are raised in Ontario. If it's not available, or if you prefer, you can substitute Cornish game hen.*

*Quails and Marinade:*

| | | |
|---|---|---|
| 6 | quails, or 4 Cornish game hens | 6 |
| ½ cup | low-fat yogurt | 125 mL |
| 2 tbsp | wine vinegar | 25 mL |
| 3 to 4 | cloves garlic | 3 to 4 |
| 1-inch | cube ginger | 2.5 cm |
| 1 | medium onion | 1 |
| 1 tsp | ground turmeric | 5 mL |
| 1 tsp | toasted ground cumin | 5 mL |
| 1 tsp | Garam Masala (p. 6) | 5 mL |
| 1 tsp | red chili powder | 5 mL |
| 1 tbsp | canned crushed tomatoes | 15 mL |
| ¼ cup | finely chopped cilantro | 50 mL |

1. Skin quail and prick meat all over with fork.
2. In food processor, blend marinade ingredients into paste. Coat each bird with marinade, putting some inside as well. Cover and marinate in refrigerator for 20 minutes or overnight. Reserve any marinade not used.
3. To cook, preheat oven to 450°F/230°C. Place birds in oven and immediately decrease heat to 350°F/180°C. Roast quail for 15 minutes, game hens for 30 minutes, or until juices run clear. Or, barbecue with rack high above coals or over a medium flame, turning often, until juices run clear.
4. In pan over high heat, combine chili powder, crushed tomatoes and remaining unused marinade. Cook for 10 minutes, stirring frequently. Add cilantro and remove from heat. Pour over quails and serve with salad and rice or naan bread.

*Serves 6*

**EACH SERVING PROVIDES:**

| | | |
|---|---|---|
| | Calories | 153 |
| g | Protein | 22 |
| g | Carbohydrates | 6 |
| g | Fibre | 1 |
| g | Fat | 5 |
| g | Saturated Fat | 1 |
| mg | Cholesterol | 66 |
| mg | Sodium | 64 |
| mg | Potassium | 336 |

Excellent: niacin, vitamin B-12, vitamin B-6
Good: thiamine, riboflavin

# Chicken Biriani

*This dish was introduced to India by the Moguls and used to celebrate Ied, the Muslim festival that celebrates the end of fasting for the month of Ramadan. It's still served on special occasions, but it also has the ability to turn any occasion into a special one. For the past 15 years we've had a very loyal customer, Jim Donnely, who always ordered this dish. It took us nine years to convert him to eating something other than Chicken Biriani!*

### Biriani Rice

Here's an everyday biriani. Soak 1 cup/250 mL basmati rice for 20 minutes. Drain, then add to 6 cups/1.5 L boiling water with ¼ tsp/1 mL lemon juice and 1 tsp/ 5 mL salt. Return to boil, then reduce heat to low and simmer covered for 10 minutes. Drain and rinse. Heat 1 tsp/5 mL oil over high heat. Add 1 cinnamon stick, 2 cloves and 2 cardamom pods. When spices pop, remove from heat and combine with rice. Fold in 1 tsp/ 15 mL crispy-fried onions. Dissolve a pinch of saffron strands in a spoonful of hot water. Sprinkle over rice. Cover and bake at 300°F/100°C for 15 minutes, or microwave for 4 minutes.

*Chicken and Marinade:*

| | | |
|---|---|---|
| ½ tsp | salt | 2 mL |
| 1 tsp | minced chilies | 5 mL |
| 1½ tsp | crushed ginger | 7 mL |
| 1½ tsp | crushed garlic | 7 mL |
| 3 to 4 lb | chicken, cut in 8 pieces (or 8 breasts) | 1.5 to 2 kg |
| 3 cups | rice | 750 mL |
| 12 cups | water | 3 L |
| 1 cup | yogurt | 250 mL |
| ⅛ | star anise (1 petal) | ⅛ |
| 4 | bay leaves | 4 |
| 2 | cardamom pods, preferably black | 2 |
| 1 | green chili, or to taste | 1 |
| 1 tsp | crushed ginger | 5 mL |
| 1 tsp | crushed garlic | 5 mL |
| 1 tbsp | vegetable oil | 15 mL |
| 2 | sticks cinnamon | 2 |
| 4 | cardamom pods | 4 |
| 4 to 6 | cloves | 4 to 6 |
| 1 | large onion, chopped | 1 |
| 2 tbsp | tomato paste | 25 mL |
| 1 tsp | salt | 5 mL |
| ¼ cup | canned crispy-fried onions | 50 mL |
| pinch | saffron threads | pinch |

1. Combine all marinade ingredients. Skin chicken and combine with marinade. Marinate for 1 to 2 hours in fridge.

See photos on cover and facing p. 36

2. Rinse rice until water runs clear. Cover with warm water and soak for 20 minutes. Drain.

3. Bring 12 cups/3L fresh water to boil. Add rice and return to boil. Reduce heat to medium and simmer uncovered until half-done (approximately 12 minutes). Remove from heat and drain. Sprinkle rice with cold water to remove stickiness.

4. In blender, combine yogurt, star anise, bay leaves, black cardamom pods, green chili, ginger and garlic. Blend until smooth and set aside.

5. Heat oil in large skillet over high heat. Add cinnamon, cardamom and cloves. When seeds start to pop, add chopped raw onion. Cook until onion is golden brown.

6. Add tomato paste, salt and yogurt mixture. Stir well and add chicken. Simmer for 7 to 8 minutes. Sprinkle half the crispy-fried onions over chicken.

7. Preheat oven to 350°F/180°C, unless you will be finishing dish on top of stove.

8. Transfer chicken to ovenproof casserole, distributing around sides and leaving centre empty. Add half the rice, filling centre and covering chicken. Sprinkle with remaining crispy onions. Add remaining rice.

9. Warm 2 or 3 tbsp/25 or 50 mL water and dissolve saffron. When water is yellow, sprinkle over top layer of rice. Cover and cook in preheated oven or over low heat on stove for 30 minutes.

10. To assemble, spoon top layer of rice around edges of warmed serving platter. Fill centre of platter with remaining rice. Place chicken pieces and any gravy on top.

*Serves 8*

**EACH SERVING PROVIDES:**

|    | Calories | 564 |
|----|----------|-----|
| g  | Protein | 53 |
| g  | Carbohydrates | 69 |
| g  | Fibre | 2 |
| g  | Fat | 8 |
| g  | Saturated Fat | 2 |
| mg | Cholesterol | 120 |
| mg | Sodium | 556 |
| mg | Potassium | 495 |

Excellent: niacin, vitamin B-12, vitamin B-6, vitamin C
Good: riboflavin, iron, zinc

# Chicken Piri Piri

*The Portuguese took chilies to Goa, about halfway down the west coast of India, and this dish is a Goan and Portuguese concoction. In Portuguese,* piri piri *means chilies. This goes well with naan bread (p. 97) and sweet rice (p. 24).*

| | | |
|---|---|---|
| 1 lb | skinless, boneless chicken breast | 500 g |
| 1½ tsp | vegetable oil | 7 mL |
| 1 | medium onion, diced | 1 |
| 1 tbsp | Chili Paste (p. 90) or minced chili | 15 mL |
| 1 tsp | ginger | 5 mL |
| 1 tsp | garlic | 5 mL |
| 1 tsp | salt | 5 mL |
| 4 tsp | canned crushed tomatoes | 20 mL |
| ½ cup | Tamarind Sauce (p. 109) or balsamic vinegar | 125 mL |
| ½ cup | water | 125 mL |
| 1 | small red or green pepper, diced | 1 |
| 1 | medium tomato, diced | 1 |

1. Cut chicken into bite-sized pieces.
2. Heat oil over high heat. Add onion and cook for 2 minutes. When onion begins to turn transparent, add chili paste. Cook for 1 minute.
3. Reduce to medium heat and add ginger, garlic, salt and crushed tomato. Add chicken and increase heat to high. Cook, stirring often, for about 5 minutes or until chicken is done. Add tamarind sauce, reduce heat to low and add water. Cook covered for 5 minutes to create sauce. Add pepper and tomato. Mix and serve.

*Serves 4*

**EACH SERVING PROVIDES:**

| | | |
|---|---|---|
| | Calories | 182 |
| g | Protein | 26 |
| g | Carbohydrates | 8 |
| g | Fibre | 2 |
| g | Fat | 5 |
| g | Saturated Fat | 1 |
| mg | Cholesterol | 67 |
| mg | Sodium | 687 |
| mg | Potassium | 362 |

Excellent: niacin
Good: vitamin B-6, vitamin C

# Chicken Jalfarezi

*This is a Chinese-Bengali dish. Chinese immigrants took their stir-frying method to India and the people of Bengal added their own spices. Together they created a healthy and very tasty dish.*

| | | |
|---|---|---|
| 1 tbsp | vegetable oil | 15 mL |
| 2 | medium onions, sliced | 2 |
| 1-inch | piece ginger | 2.5 cm |
| 4 to 6 | cloves garlic | 4 to 6 |
| 1½ tsp | salt | 7 mL |
| 1 tsp | crushed red chili, or to taste | 5 mL |
| 1 tbsp | canned crushed tomatoes | 15 mL |
| 1 lb | chicken tenders or boneless breast or pork (cubed) | 500 g |
| 2 cups | fresh vegetables (cauliflower, broccoli, carrots, etc.) | 500 mL |
| ½ | green pepper, diced | ½ |
| ½ | red pepper, diced | ½ |
| 2 | medium tomatoes, diced | 2 |

1. Heat oil over medium heat. Add onions and cook until soft. Add ginger and garlic and stir for 2 minutes. Reduce heat to medium and add salt, red chili and crushed tomato. Cook and stir for 3 minutes.
2. Increase heat to high and add chicken. When chicken has changed colour and is half-cooked (about 4 minutes), add vegetables. Reduce heat to medium and cook covered for 8 to 10 minutes, until vegetables are tender.
3. Lift cover and add peppers and tomato. Stir, remove from heat and serve. (To serve over rice, you may want to make more gravy by adding chicken stock or low-fat yogurt to sauce at the end, and cooking for 2 to 3 minutes.)

*Serves 4*

**EACH SERVING PROVIDES:**

| | | |
|---|---|---|
| | Calories | 220 |
| g | Protein | 28 |
| g | Carbohydrates | 13 |
| g | Fibre | 3 |
| g | Fat | 7 |
| g | Saturated Fat | 1 |
| mg | Cholesterol | 67 |
| mg | Sodium | 876 |
| mg | Potassium | 594 |

Excellent: niacin, vitamin B-6, vitamin C, folacin

# Chicken Curry

*Indians tend to use the word "curry" to describe sauce. In North America, "curry" is firmly established as a spicy stew like this one. Curries don't have to be hot. You can reduce or eliminate the chili, ginger, black pepper and similar hot spices and still enjoy delicious flavour.*

| | | |
|---|---|---|
| 1 lb | skinless, boneless chicken breast | 500 g |
| 2 tsp | vegetable oil | 10 mL |
| 2-to-3-inch | cinnamon stick | 5-to-7.5 cm |
| 4 | cloves | 4 |
| 2 | cardamom pods | 2 |
| 2 | medium onions, finely chopped | 2 |
| 1½ tsp | crushed garlic | 7 mL |
| 1½ tsp | crushed ginger | 7 mL |
| 2 | green chilies or to taste, crushed and diced | 2 |
| 1½ tsp | Meat Masala (p. 5) | 7 mL |
| ½ tsp | ground turmeric | 2 mL |
| 1 tsp | salt | 5 mL |
| 2 | medium tomatoes, skinned | 2 |
| 1 tbsp | tomato paste | 15 mL |
| 1 tbsp | low-fat yogurt | 15 mL |
| 4 cups | water | 1 L |
| 2 | medium potatoes, cut in 8 pieces each | 2 |
| 1 tbsp | finely chopped cilantro | 15 mL |

**EACH SERVING PROVIDES:**

| | | |
|---|---|---|
| | Calories | 245 |
| g | Protein | 28 |
| g | Carbohydrates | 21 |
| g | Fibre | 3 |
| g | Fat | 6 |
| g | Saturated Fat | 1 |
| mg | Cholesterol | 21 |
| mg | Sodium | 908 |
| mg | Potassium | 743 |

Excellent: niacin, vitamin B-6, vitamin C

Good: iron, zinc

1. Cut chicken into bite-sized pieces.
2. Heat oil in heavy non-stick pot over high heat. Add cinnamon, cloves and cardamom. When seeds start to pop, add onions. Saute onions until golden brown. Add garlic, ginger, chilies, meat masala, turmeric and salt. Reduce heat to low and add fresh tomatoes. Cook covered for 5 minutes or until a chunky sauce has formed. Add chicken.
3. Whisk together tomato paste and yogurt and add to pot. Increase heat to high and stir until boiling. Add water and potatoes and cook covered for 5 to 6 minutes, or until potatoes are tender. Add cilantro before serving. Bread or rice and onion salad make a nice accompaniment.

*Serves 4*

# Cumin Chicken
## JEERA CHICKEN

*This isn't a traditional dish. It was created in London by a Ugandan chef who moved there. I have introduced it in my cooking classes and it's been a big hit. Seeing it's not traditional anyway, why not experiment? Try it with turkey breast.*

*Chicken and Marinade:*

| | | |
|---|---|---|
| ½ tsp | salt | 2 mL |
| 1 tsp | crushed ginger | 5 mL |
| 1 tsp | crushed garlic | 5 mL |
| 1½ tsp | vegetable oil | 7 mL |
| 3-to-4-lb | whole chicken, or 8 to 12 chicken pieces | 1.5 to 2 kg |
| | | |
| 2 tsp | crushed garlic | 10 mL |
| 2 tsp | crushed ginger | 10 mL |
| ½ tsp | salt | 2 mL |
| 1 to 2 | green chilies, or to taste | 1 to 2 |
| 1 tbsp | ground cumin | 15 mL |
| 1 tbsp | vegetable oil | 15 mL |
| 1 | medium onion, sliced | 1 |

1. Cut chicken into 8 to 12 pieces and remove skin. Combine marinade ingredients and toss with chicken pieces to coat. Marinate in fridge for 8 hours or longer.
2. In blender, blend garlic, ginger, salt, green chilies and cumin to paste. A little water may be needed.
3. Heat oil in non-stick skillet over high heat. Add onion and cook until transparent. Add blender mixture and stir well. Add chicken with marinade and cook covered until chicken is tender, about 20 minutes. Serve with potatoes and steamed carrots.

*Serves 4*

**EACH SERVING PROVIDES:**

| | | |
|---|---|---|
| | Calories | 531 |
| g | Protein | 90 |
| g | Carbohydrates | 5 |
| g | Fibre | 2 |
| g | Fat | 15 |
| g | Saturated Fat | 3 |
| mg | Cholesterol | 238 |
| mg | Sodium | 730 |
| mg | Potassium | 695 |

Excellent: niacin, vitamin B-12, vitamin B-6, iron, zinc
Good: riboflavin, vitamin C, vitamin D

# Chicken Masala

*One day when we had visitors, I had undertaken to cook five hares my husband had shot. He went out with the men and we women stayed behind. Indian women don't usually eat rabbit or hare, but these were so tempting that we ate them all! I sent out for five chickens and cooked them in the same sauce, or masala. My husband and I had a good laugh about it, and he named this dish.*

| | | |
|---|---|---|
| 2-inch | cube ginger | 5 cm |
| 6 to 8 | cloves garlic | 6 to 8 |
| ½ tsp | salt | 2 mL |
| 1 tsp | red chili powder, or to taste | 5 mL |
| 1 lb | skinless, boneless chicken breasts | 500 g |
| | | |
| 1 cup | canned crushed tomatoes | 250 mL |
| 2 | green chilies, or to taste | 2 |
| 1 cup | canned whole plum tomatoes | 250 mL |
| 1 bunch | cilantro, chopped | 1 bunch |
| 1 tbsp | vegetable oil | 15 mL |
| 1 | medium onion, finely chopped | 1 |
| 1 tsp | Meat Masala (p. 5) | 5 mL |
| 1 tsp | ground turmeric | 5 mL |
| 1 tsp | salt | 5 mL |
| 1 cup | low-fat yogurt, stirred smooth | 250 mL |

1. In blender, puree ginger and garlic with a little water to thick paste.
2. To make marinade, mix 2 tbsp/25 mL of garlic-ginger mixture with salt and chili powder. Cut chicken breast into bite-sized pieces, toss with marinade to coat and marinate in refrigerator for 20 to 30 minutes.
3. In food processor, finely chop crushed tomato and green chilies. Add plum tomatoes and cilantro and quickly mix leaving tomatoes chunky.
4. Heat oil in large skillet over medium heat. Sear chicken, remove from pan and set aside. Add onion and cook until golden. Add remaining ginger-garlic mixture and cook for 2 minutes. Add meat masala, turmeric, salt and tomato mixture. Stir in yogurt. Cook, stirring, for 10 to 15 minutes. Add chicken and cook for 10 to 15 minutes or until chicken is tender.

*Serves 4*

## Red chili powder

Chili powder is made from the ripe chili fruit. First it's dried in the sun and both the skin and seeds are ground into powder. Red chili powder is hot, so use it sparingly or according to taste.

Don't confuse chili powder with chili con carne powder, which is a combination of chili powder, cumin and other spices.

### EACH SERVING PROVIDES:

| | | |
|---|---|---|
| | Calories | 282 |
| g | Protein | 32 |
| g | Carbohydrates | 22 |
| g | Fibre | 4 |
| g | Fat | 8 |
| g | Saturated Fat | 2 |
| mg | Cholesterol | 71 |
| mg | Sodium | 796 |
| mg | Potassium | 983 |

Excellent: niacin, vitamin B-12, vitamin B-6, vitamin C, vitamin E, phosphorus
Good: vitamin A, thiamine B1, riboflavin, folacin, calcium, iron, zinc

# Karahi Chicken with Vegetables

*Karahi is an Indian wok. This way of cooking is popular in the Himalayan mountain region and surrounding areas. The spices are different from Pakistan to Afghanistan to China, but the cooking method is the same. The aroma of this recipe will travel from the kitchen to the farthest corner of the house and will bring everybody to the dining table.*

| | | |
|---|---|---|
| 1 lb | chicken tenders, or skinless, boneless chicken breast | 500 g |
| 4 to 6 | cloves garlic | 4 to 6 |
| 2-inch | cube ginger | 5 cm |
| 1 tbsp | vegetable oil | 15 mL |
| 1 cup | sliced onions | 250 mL |
| 1 tsp | salt | 5 mL |
| | Chili Paste (p. 90) or minced chilies to taste | |
| 4 tbsp | canned crushed tomatoes | 20 mL |
| 1 cup | fresh vegetables in bite-sized pieces (carrots, broccoli, cauliflower, beans, etc.) | 250 mL |
| 2 tbsp | low-fat yogurt | 25 mL |
| 2 | medium tomatoes, diced (1 cup/250 mL) | 2 |
| 1 | medium green or red pepper | 1 |
| 2 tsp | powdered dried fenugreek leaves (kasuri methi) (optional) | 10 mL |

1. Cut chicken into bite-sized pieces and set aside.
2. Finely chop garlic and ginger and set aside.
3. Heat oil over high heat in large skillet or wok. Add onion and cook until golden brown. Add ginger and garlic and cook for 2 minutes. Add salt, chili paste and crushed tomato. Cook for 2 minutes and add chicken. Cook for 4 more minutes and add vegetables. Cook for 3 minutes until chicken is firm and opaque. Add yogurt and mix well.
4. Reduce heat to medium, add fresh tomatoes, bell pepper and dried fenugreek leaves. Mix and cook covered for 2 minutes until peppers are just tender. Serve with naan bread (p. 97) and boiled rice.

*Serves 4*

## Stir-fries

**Stir-frying vegetables in a non-stick skillet or wok uses only a little oil and helps them retain their crunch and their vitamin content. By constantly stirring and tossing the contents of the pan over high heat, you coat them to seal in flavour and cook them quickly to maintian their texture. You can even eliminate oil altogether by using a little stock or wine instead—just keep adding small amounts during cooking to keep the contents of the pan from sticking.**

**EACH SERVING PROVIDES:**

| | | |
|---|---|---|
| | Calories | 214 |
| g | Protein | 28 |
| g | Carbohydrates | 11 |
| g | Fibre | 2 |
| g | Fat | 7 |
| g | Saturated Fat | 1 |
| mg | Cholesterol | 68 |
| mg | Sodium | 622 |
| mg | Potassium | 502 |

Excellent: niacin, vitamin C
Good: vitamin B-6, folacin, vitamin E

# Indian Christmas Turkey

*Roast Turkey*
**The fat in poultry skin flavours the meat and keeps it from drying out during cooking. Unfortunately, it also adds fat. But if you cook the poultry with the skin on, and then remove it before serving, you can have all the advantages of the skin and none of the disadvantages. If spices are involved, slit the skin and rub them through, or rub them under the skin so they flavour the meat.**

*Indian converts to Christianity have adapted the traditional turkey dinner for occasions like Christmas. I started cooking turkey in our restaurant in London for these special occasions and I have maintained the tradition by cooking turkey in Vancouver too. Some customers treat themselves to turkey dinner many times in the season.*

*Turkey and Marinade:*

| | | |
|---|---|---|
| 1 cup | low-fat yogurt | 250 mL |
| 3 tsp | crushed garlic | 15 mL |
| 3 tsp | crushed ginger | 15 mL |
| 2 tsp | paprika | 10 mL |
| 2 tsp | Chili Paste (p. 90) or minced chili | 10 mL |
| 1 tsp | salt | 5 mL |
| 6 | thin slices underripe papaya, (½ cup/125 mL) or kiwi fruit | 6 |
| 8-lb | turkey | 4 kg |

*Stuffing:*

| | | |
|---|---|---|
| 1 tsp | vegetable oil | 5 mL |
| 2 | medium onions, sliced | 2 |
| 2 | 1-inch/2.5 cm cinnamon sticks | 2 |
| 6 | cloves | 6 |
| 6 | cardamom pods | 6 |
| 2 tsp | cumin seeds | 10 mL |
| 1 tsp | crushed ginger | 5 mL |
| 2 tsp | crushed garlic | 10 mL |
| 3 to 4 cups | cooked basmati or other long-grain rice | 750 mL to 1 L |
| 1 cup | frozen mixed vegetables, thawed | 250 mL |
| ½ | green pepper, diced | ½ |
| ½ | red pepper, diced | ½ |
| | juice of 1 large lemon | |
| 1 tbsp | tomato paste | 15 mL |
| 1 tbsp | cornstarch | 15 mL |
| 1 cup | canned crushed tomatoes | 250 mL |

1. Blend marinade ingredients in blender.
2. Prepare turkey by making a few parallel deep cuts on each part so spices will flavour meat. Cover turkey inside and out with marinade and marinate in fridge for 12 hours.
3. Preheat oven to 400°F/200°C.
4. To prepare stuffing, heat oil in large pan over high heat. Add onions and cook until soft. Add cinnamon, cloves, cardamom pods, cumin, ginger and garlic and cook for 2 minutes or until fragrant. Add rice, vegetables, green and red pepper and lemon juice. Mix well and remove from heat.
5. Stuff turkey and roast uncovered for approximately 15 minutes per pound. Basting is not necessary.
6. When turkey is ready, remove from oven and drain juices into large bowl. Tent turkey with foil and leave at room temperature for at least 10 minutes. Skim off fat layer that forms on top of juices.
7. Place large pan over high heat and add skimmed juices. Combine cornstarch with a little water and mix with tomato paste and crushed tomatoes. Add to juices, bring to boil and reduce, stirring, to thick gravy. Serve with turkey.

*Serves 15*

**EACH SERVING PROVIDES:**

|    | Calories      | 299 |
|----|---------------|-----|
| g  | Protein       | 38  |
| g  | Carbohydrates | 19  |
| g  | Fibre         | 1   |
| g  | Fat           | 7   |
| g  | Saturated Fat | 2   |
| mg | Cholesterol   | 92  |
| mg | Sodium        | 388 |
| mg | Potassium     | 500 |

Excellent: niacin, vitamin B-12, vitamin B5, vitamin D, zinc

Good: riboflavin, iron

# Tandoori Chicken

A tandoor *is a clay oven that looks like a waist-high jug with a charcoal fire in the bottom. Clay ovens have been used in the Middle East since time immemorial to bake bread. The Indians, especially from the North, started cooking chicken and meat in the tandoor, and it's delicious, partly because of the marinades and the infusion of smoke (created from drippings).*

*The closest thing we have in North America is the barbecue. During barbecue season you can use skinless, boneless chicken. Put the pieces on skewers and barbecue, turning, as you would a steak or lamb chops. Game, rabbit, lamb or any other meat can be substituted for chicken with this same marinade.*

| | | |
|---|---|---|
| ½ cup | low-fat yogurt | 125 mL |
| 1 tsp | salt | 5 mL |
| ½-inch | cube ginger | 1 cm |
| 3 | cloves garlic | 3 |
| 2 tsp | ground cumin | 10 mL |
| ¼ tsp | mustard powder | 1 mL |
| 1 tsp | vegetable oil | 5 mL |
| ½ tsp | Chili Paste (p. 90) or minced chili | 2 mL |
| | 1 or 2 drops reddish golden food colour (optional) | |
| 3-to-4-lb | skinless whole chicken, cut in 4 pieces, or 4 large skinless pieces | 1.5-to-2 kg |

1. Puree yogurt, salt, ginger, garlic, cumin, mustard, oil, chili paste and food colour (if desired) and blend into paste.
2. Clean and prepare chicken by making deep cuts. Coat completely with paste and marinate in refrigerator for 2 hours or longer.
3. Tandoori chicken is traditionally barbecued in a clay oven but you can bake it in preheated oven at 400°F/200°C for 30 minutes, then brown under broiler for 5 minutes.
   Or, to barbecue, cook slowly, either with grill raised high above coals or over medium flame so chicken will be cooked through.

*Serves 4*

From top: Balti Vegetables (p. 38), Chapatis (p. 100), Beef Curry (p. 61)

# Fish & Seafood

❩ *indicates hot dishes*

From top: Raita (p. 112), Naan Bread (p. 97), Pulao Rice (p. 23), Fish with Cilantro and Mint (p. 88)

# Fish Tikka

*The people on both coasts of India, Sri Lanka and Sindh–Pakistan use rock salmon for this recipe. It's an Indian Ocean fish that looks like red snapper but is almost identical in taste and texture to halibut. Use a firm-fleshed fish that won't fall apart when cooked.*

*Marinade:*

| | | |
|---|---|---|
| 1 tbsp | low-fat yogurt | 15 mL |
| 1 tbsp | vegetable oil | 15 mL |
| ½ tsp | crushed ginger | 2 mL |
| ½ tsp | crushed garlic | 2 mL |
| 1 tsp | Chili Paste (p. 90) or minced chili | 5 mL |
| 1 tsp | ground cumin | 5 mL |
| 1 tsp | salt | 5 mL |
| | | |
| 1 lb | halibut or other firm-fleshed white fish | 500 g |
| | vegetable oil spray | |

1. In blender, blend marinade ingredients to thick paste.
2. Cut fish into 8 equal pieces. Combine fish and marinade and marinate in fridge for 2 hours.
3. Preheat oven to 400°F/200°C, or start barbecue. For baking, lightly coat baking pan with vegetable oil spray. Place fish on baking pan and bake for 10 minutes. Drain any liquid, turn fish over and bake for 10 more minutes.

   Or, barbecue for 10 minutes. Serve with raita (p. 112) and a salad of any sort. Naan bread (p. 97) is also a good accompaniment.

*Serves 4*

**EACH SERVING PROVIDES:**

| | | |
|---|---|---|
| | Calories | 130 |
| g | Protein | 21 |
| g | Carbohydrates | 1 |
| g | Fibre | trace |
| g | Fat | 4 |
| g | Saturated Fat | 1 |
| mg | Cholesterol | 49 |
| mg | Sodium | 604 |
| mg | Potassium | 501 |

Excellent: vitamin B-12, vitamin D
Good: vitamin B-6, vitamin E

# Bengali Fish

*Since the only non-vegetarian item in the Bengalis' diet is fish, they have some wonderful fish dishes. Traditionally these recipes use large quantities of oil and coconut. This is a delightfully simple, tasty HeartSmart alternative.*

*Fish and Marinade:*

| | | |
|---|---|---|
| ½ cup | water | 125 mL |
| 1 tsp | salt | 5 mL |
| 1 tsp | ground turmeric | 5 mL |
| 1 tsp | mustard powder or Dijon mustard | 5 mL |
| ½ tsp | red chili powder, or to taste | 2 mL |
| 2 tsp | lemon juice | 10 mL |
| 1½ lb | cod or any white fish, cut in 4 equal pieces | 750 g |
| | | |
| 1 cup | water, for steaming | 250 mL |
| 3 | green chilies (or to taste), sliced | 3 |
| ½ cup | cilantro | 125 mL |

1. To prepare marinade, combine water, salt, turmeric, mustard, chili powder and lemon juice in mixing bowl. Mix well and add fish. Marinate in refrigerator for 30 minutes.
2. Heat 1 cup/250 mL water in bottom of steamer. Place fish over water in steamer basket, cover with green chilies and steam for 15 minutes. Juices will create sauce in bottom part of steamer. If you need more add some hot water. (Fish can also be placed directly in water and poached. Keep water at low simmer.) Garnish with cilantro and serve over rice.

*Serves 4*

**EACH SERVING PROVIDES:**

| | | |
|---|---|---|
| | Calories | 144 |
| g | Protein | 25 |
| g | Carbohydrates | 4 |
| g | Fibre | 1 |
| g | Fat | 3 |
| g | Saturated Fat | trace |
| mg | Cholesterol | 24 |
| mg | Sodium | 632 |
| mg | Potassium | 662 |

Excellent: niacin, vitamin B-12, vitamin C, vitamin D
Good: vitamin B-6

# Fish with Cilantro and Mint

See photo, p. 85

*Finding Fresh Fish*
**Buy fish that has firm flesh—if your finger leaves a lingering dent after you touch it, it's too old. And fresh fish doesn't have that fishy smell—that's a sign it's been out of the water too long. Fresh fish should be refrigerated and used within 2 or 3 days.**

*My brother-in-law spent some time in Nigeria where he met a Sindhi family from Hyderabad-Sindh in Pakistan. It was at their house that he first tasted this regional specialty, and he introduced it to us.*

| | | |
|---|---|---|
| 6 | cloves garlic | 6 |
| 1-inch | cube ginger | 2.5 cm |
| 2 tbsp | canned crushed tomatoes | 25 mL |
| 1 bunch | cilantro | 1 bunch |
| 4 | small green chilies, or to taste | 4 |
| 4 tsp | vegetable oil | 20 mL |
| 1½ lb | cod, halibut or other firm-fleshed white fish | 750 g |
| 1 | medium onion, sliced | 1 |
| 4 tsp | Dhania-jeera (p. 6) or mild curry powder | 20 mL |
| ½ tsp | ground turmeric | 2 mL |
| 1 tsp | salt | 5 ml |
| ½ | lemon | ½ |
| 3 to 4 tsp | Mint Chutney | 15 to 20 mL |

1. In food processor, crush garlic, ginger, tomato, cilantro and chilies.
2. Heat oil in shallow pan over high heat. Add fish and cook, turning once, until fish flakes easily. Remove to plate and keep warm.
3. Add onion to pan and stir-fry until tender. Add dhania-jeera masala, turmeric, salt and processor mixture. Bring to boil and cook for 5 minutes, stirring constantly. Add fish and cook to reduce sauce, about 2 minutes. Spoon mint chutney over top and squeeze on lemon juice.

*Mint Chutney*

| | | |
|---|---|---|
| 1 | small onion | 1 |
| 1 cup | mint leaves | 250 mL |
| 1 tsp | lemon juice | 5 mL |
| 1 tsp | sugar | 5 mL |
| pinch | salt | pinch |

1. In blender, blend all ingredients to consistency of ketchup.

*Serves 4*

**EACH SERVING PROVIDES:**

| | | |
|---|---|---|
| | Calories | 221 |
| g | Protein | 24 |
| g | Carbohydrates | 19 |
| g | Fibre | 5 |
| g | Fat | 7 |
| g | Saturated Fat | 1 |
| mg | Cholesterol | 49 |
| mg | Sodium | 814 |
| mg | Potassium | 1004 |

Excellent: vitamin B-12, vitamin B-6, vitamin C, vitamin D, vitamin E, iron
Good: vitamin A, thiamine, niacin, folacin, calcium
See photo, p. 85

# Steamed Salmon in Banana Leaf

*Wrapping food in leaves is common to many of the world's cuisines. The banana leaf imparts a very distinct flavour which steaming intensifies. If you don't have Asian or Caribbean stores nearby, use spinach, endive, lettuce or even grape leaves. Cooking parchment also works.*

| | | |
|---|---|---|
| ½ cup | 1% milk | 125 mL |
| 1 tsp | fine unsweetened coconut | 5 mL |
| ¼ cup | chopped mint | 50 mL |
| 4 | cloves garlic, crushed | 4 |
| 1 tsp | ground cumin | 5 mL |
| 4 | green chilies, crushed, or to taste | 4 |
| 2 tsp | lemon juice | 10 mL |
| 1½ lb | salmon or cod steaks cut in 4 pieces | 750 g |
| 2 | banana leaves halved, or sufficient other edible leaves, or parchment to wrap 4 servings | 2 |
| ½ tsp | salt | 2 mL |
| ½ tsp | pepper | 2 ml |
| ¾ cup | water | 175 mL |
| ¼ cup | vinegar | 50 mL |
| 8 | dried curry leaves or 4 bay leaves | 8 |

1. Combine milk, coconut, mint, garlic, cumin, green chilies and lemon juice. Let sit for 10 minutes to soak coconut.
2. Dry fish on paper towel. Place each piece in centre of banana leaf or parchment. Sprinkle with salt and pepper and let sit for 5 minutes.
3. Spoon coconut mixture over fish. Fold leaf and tie with kitchen string. (If using parchment, make package that encloses fish completely but leaves enough space for steam to infuse its aroma.)
4. Heat water with vinegar and curry leaves in pot large enough to hold vegetable steamer. Bring to boil, put fish packets in steamer over water and steam covered for 15 minutes. Serve immediately.

*Serves 4*

## Omega 3 Fatty Acids

**Fatty fish, such as salmon, mackerel and trout contain omega 3 fatty acids. These fish oils may reduce your risk of heart disease by reducing the clotting tendency of blood.**

**EACH SERVING PROVIDES:**

| | | |
|---|---|---|
| | Calories | 141 |
| g | Protein | 16 |
| g | Carbohydrates | 16 |
| g | Fibre | 5 |
| g | Fat | 2 |
| g | Saturated Fat | 1 |
| mg | Cholesterol | 26 |
| mg | Sodium | 368 |
| mg | Potassium | 493 |

Excellent: vitamin B-6, vitamin C, calcium, iron
Good: vitamin D

# Fish Vindaloo

*The Goans, under Portugese influence, introduced vindaloo to Indian cuisine. A vindaloo can be chicken, beef or fish. Whatever, it's one of the hottest dishes on the Indian subcontinent. Serve it with rice, a sweet chutney and a yogurt sauce or drink (raita or lassi) to cool it down.*

Fish and Marinade:

| | | |
|---|---|---|
| 1½ lb | halibut or other firm-fleshed white fish | 750 g |
| ½ tsp | salt | 2 mL |
| 1 tbsp | lemon juice | 15 mL |
| | vegetable oil spray | |
| | | |
| 1 tsp | vegetable oil | 5 mL |
| ½ tsp | mustard seeds | 2 mL |
| ½ | medium onion, chopped | ½ |
| 1 tsp | crushed garlic | 5 mL |
| ½ tsp | ground turmeric | 2 mL |
| 2 tsp | Chili Paste (p. 90) or minced chili, or to taste | 10 mL |
| 2 tsp | Dhania-jeera Masala (p. 6) or mild curry powder | 10 mL |
| 1 | fresh tomato, chopped | 1 |
| 2 tsp | Tamarind Sauce (p. 109) or balsamic vinegar | 10 mL |
| 3 tsp | brown sugar | 15 mL |
| 2 cups | water | 500 mL |
| ½ cup | cilantro | 125 mL |
| 1 tsp | salt | 5 mL |

1. Cut fish into 1 inch/2.5 cm chunks. Mix salt and lemon juice. Toss fish with marinade to coat and marinate for 15 minutes.
2. Lightly coat non-stick pan with vegetable oil spray and place over medium heat. Add fish and cook until almost done (about 2 minutes per side). Set aside.
3. Return pan to high heat and heat oil. Add mustard seeds. When seeds start to pop, add onion and saute until golden brown. Add garlic and saute for 2 minutes. Add turmeric, chili paste, dhania-jeera masala and fresh tomato. Reduce heat to low and cook for 5 minutes, until tomato is softened.

4. Add tamarind sauce, brown sugar and water. Increase heat to high and bring to boil. Boil for 10 minutes to thicken sauce. Remove from heat, add cilantro and puree mixture in blender (add some water if sauce is too thick).

5. Return pan to high heat. Pour blender mixture back into pan and heat. Add fish and salt. Cook for 5 minutes, or until fish is opaque all through, and serve.

*Serves 4*

**EACH SERVING PROVIDES:**

|    |                | |
|----|----------------|-----|
|    | Calories       | 179 |
| g  | Protein        | 25  |
| g  | Carbohydrates  | 9   |
| g  | Fibre          | 2   |
| g  | Fat            | 5   |
| g  | Saturated Fat  | 1   |
| mg | Cholesterol    | 36  |
| mg | Sodium         | 888 |
| mg | Potassium      | 717 |

Excellent: niacin, vitamin D
Good: vitamin B-6, iron

# Madras Prawns

*In Madras, on the southeast coast of India, you find very hot food. In fact, it's lent its name to the classic hot spice mixture Madras curry powder. The region is called Tamil Nadu now, but the curry will always be called Madras.*

*Prawns and Marinade:*

| | | |
|---|---|---|
| 1 lb | headless prawns, peeled and deveined | 500 g |
| ½ tsp | crushed garlic | 2 mL |
| ½ tsp | Chili Paste (p. 90) or minced chili, or to taste | 2 mL |
| ½ tsp | salt | 2 mL |
| | | |
| 1 tsp | vegetable oil | 5 mL |
| 1 | medium onion, chopped | 1 |
| ½ tsp | crushed garlic | 2 mL |
| ½ tsp | Chili Paste (p. 90) or minced chili, or to taste | 2 mL |
| 1 tbsp | canned crushed tomatoes | 15 mL |
| ½ tsp | salt | 2 mL |
| ½ tsp | Dhania-jeera Masala (p. 6) or mild curry powder | 2 mL |
| ¼ tsp | turmeric | 1 mL |
| 1 tsp | wine vinegar | 5 mL |
| ½ | green pepper, diced | ½ |
| ½ | red pepper, diced | ½ |
| 1 | medium tomato, diced | 1 |
| ½ tsp | Garam Masala (p. 6) | 2 mL |

**EACH SERVING PROVIDES:**

| | | |
|---|---|---|
| | Calories | 126 |
| g | Protein | 18 |
| g | Carbohydrates | 7 |
| g | Fibre | 2 |
| g | Fat | 3 |
| g | Saturated Fat | trace |
| mg | Cholesterol | 161 |
| mg | Sodium | 731 |
| mg | Potassium | 349 |

Excellent: vitamin B-12, vitamin C, vitamin D, iron
Good: vitamin A, zinc

1. To make marinade, mix garlic, chili paste and salt. Toss prawns with marinade and marinate in fridge for 20 minutes.
2. Heat oil in large pan over high heat. Add onion and stir-fry until tender. Add garlic, chili paste, crushed tomatoes, salt, dhania-jeera masala and turmeric. Cook for 2 minutes. Add vinegar, peppers and diced tomato. Mix, then add garam masala and prawns. Cook for 3 to 4 minutes until prawns are uniformly pink and tender. Do not overcook. Remove from heat. Keep covered for a few minutes and serve.

*Serves 4*

# Prawn Masala

*We have Italian customers who take out our sauces for their pasta. Leftover sauce from this is the beginning of a great pasta dish the next day. Add some boiled potatoes and steamed vegetables for another full meal.*

| | | |
|---|---|---|
| 1 lb | headless prawns, peeled and deveined | 500 g |
| 2 cups | cold water | 500 mL |
| ½ tsp | lemon juice | 2 mL |
| ½ tsp | salt | 2 mL |
| | | |
| 1-inch | piece ginger | 2.5 cm |
| 4 to 6 | cloves garlic | 4 to 6 |
| 2 cups | canned plum tomatoes | 500 g |
| 1 tsp | minced green chilies, or to taste | 5 mL |
| 1 bunch | cilantro | 1 bunch |
| 1 tbsp | vegetable oil | 15 mL |
| 1 | medium onion, finely chopped | 1 |
| 1 tsp | Meat Masala (p. 5) | 5 mL |
| 1 tsp | ground turmeric | 5 mL |
| 1 tsp | salt | 5 mL |
| 1 tsp | red chili powder | 5 mL |
| 1 cup | canned crushed tomatoes | 250 mL |
| 1 cup | low-fat yogurt, stirred smooth | 250 mL |

1. Soak prawns in water, lemon and salt for 10 minutes. Drain.
2. In blender, puree ginger and garlic with some water to smooth paste.
3. In food processor, combine plum tomatoes, green chilies and cilantro and chop coarsely (tomatoes should remain chunky).
4. Heat oil over high heat in large skillet. Add onion and stir-fry until golden. Add ginger-garlic mixture and saute for 2 minutes. Add meat masala, turmeric, salt, chili powder, tomato mixture and crushed tomatoes. Mix well, add yogurt and stir for 10 to 15 minutes. Reduce heat to low and simmer, stirring occasionally, for 30 minutes to reduce.
5. Add prawns and cook for 4 to 5 minutes, until prawns are uniformly pink and tender. Serve immediately. Goes well with rice or naan bread.

*Serves 4*

**EACH SERVING PROVIDES:**

| | | |
|---|---|---|
| | Calories | 206 |
| g | Protein | 20 |
| g | Carbohydrates | 19 |
| g | Fibre | 3 |
| g | Fat | 6 |
| g | Saturated Fat | 1 |
| mg | Cholesterol | 138 |
| mg | Sodium | 757 |
| mg | Potassium | 835 |

Excellent: vitamin B-12, Vitain C, vitamin D, vitamin E, iron
Good: vitamin A, riboflavin, vitamin B-6, folacin, calcium, zinc

# Prawn Biriani

*This biriani is adapted for the people on the coast.*

### Fresh Prawns

**Fresh prawns will taste even fresher if you soak them for a few minutes in cold water with a little lemon juice and salt after you've peeled them. Use 2 cups/500 mL water and ½ tsp/2 mL each of lemon juice and salt.**

*Prawns and Marinade:*

| | | |
|---|---|---|
| 1 lb | headless prawns, peeled and deveined | 500 g |
| 2 cups | cold water | 500 mL |
| ½ tsp | lemon juice | 2 mL |
| ½ tsp | salt | 2 ml |
| 1 tsp | crushed garlic | 5 mL |
| ½ tsp | Chili Paste (p. 90) or minced chili | 1 mL |
| | | |
| 1 | medium potato | 1 |
| ½ cup | low-fat yogurt | 125 mL |
| 1 tbsp | tomato paste | 15 mL |
| ½-inch | piece ginger | 1 cm |
| 2 to 4 | cloves garlic | 2 to 4 |
| ⅛ | star anise (1 petal) | ⅛ |
| 2 | cardamom pods | 2 |
| 2 | bay leaves | 2 |
| 1 tbsp | vegetable oil | 15 mL |
| 1 | large onion, sliced | 1 |
| pinch | Garam Masala (p. 6) | pinch |
| 1 | lemon, cut in wedges for garnish | 1 |
| 1 tbsp | chopped cilantro, for garnish | 15 mL |

1. Soak prawns in water, lemon and salt for 10 minutes. Drain.
2. Mix garlic and chili paste and cover prawns. Marinate for 1 hour.
3. Cook potato. Set aside to cool. Peel and cut into bite-sized pieces.
4. In blender, puree yogurt, tomato paste, ginger, garlic, star anise, cardamom and bay leaves. Set aside.
5. In medium skillet, heat oil over high heat. Add onion and cook until golden brown. Add blender mixture. Bring to boil, stirring constantly, to thicken. Add potato and cook for 5 minutes. Add prawns and cook until uniformly pink and tender (4 minutes). Remove from heat, sprinkle with garam masala and garnish. Serve over biriani rice (p. 74).

*Serves 4*

### EACH SERVING PROVIDES:

*(analysis with 3 oz/90 g rice per person)*

| | | |
|---|---|---|
| | Calories | 319 |
| g | Protein | 29 |
| g | Carbohydrates | 37 |
| g | Fibre | 1 |
| g | Fat | 6 |
| g | Saturated Fat | 1 |
| mg | Cholesterol | 223 |
| mg | Sodium | 580 |
| mg | Potassium | 583 |

Excellent: vitamin B-12, Vitain D, iron, zinc
Good: niacin, vitamin B-6, vitamin E

# Indian Breads

# Millet Bread
## BAJRE KI ROTI

*Since he was a boy my husband has loved the wonderful flavour of millet bread, so I had my mother-in-law teach me how to make it. In the state of Gujarat, farmers eat this bread with onions for lunch. These farmers are considered the healthiest people in the area.*

*If you avoid wheat for any reason you can use all millet flour instead of the wheat-millet combination called for in this recipe.*

| | | |
|---|---|---|
| 1 cup | millet flour | 250 mL |
| 1 tbsp | whole wheat flour | 15 mL |
| pinch | salt | pinch |
| 1 tsp | vegetable oil | 5 mL |
| ½ cup | water | 125 mL |
| | vegetable oil spray | |

1. Combine dry ingredients and stir in oil. When oil is incorporated, stir in water. Knead into stiff dough. Divide into 4 equal balls. Place each ball on waxed paper. Wet hands to prevent sticking. Gently press down and turn hand in circular motion for even thickness. Make into ¼-inch-thick/5 mm patty.
2. Spray heavy griddle or skillet with vegetable oil and wipe off excess. Heat over medium heat. Gently invert 1 patty dough side down in skillet making sure there is no trapped air underneath. Lift paper off. Seal any cracks on top by stroking in circular motion with wet hand (one direction only). When one side is browned, turn over and cook other side.

*Serves 4*

## Millet

Millet is an ancient grain and a staple for almost one-third of the world's population, but North Americans are more likely to use these tiny round grains for birdseed than for dinner. Millet contains more protein than wheat or rice and it's a source of iron and calcium. For people who are allergic to wheat or just want an alternative, millet is a good, tasty substitute.

### EACH SERVING PROVIDES:

| | | |
|---|---|---|
| | Calories | 464 |
| g | Protein | 14 |
| g | Carbohydrates | 91 |
| g | Fibre | 5 |
| g | Fat | 5 |
| g | Saturated Fat | 1 |
| mg | Cholesterol | 0 |
| mg | Sodium | 202 |
| mg | Potassium | 241 |

Excellent: thiamine
Good: riboflavin, naicin equivalent, vitamin B-6, folacin, vitamin E, iron

# Classic Indian Flatbread
## NAAN

*The people of North Africa and the Middle East eat naan the way westerners eat regular leavened bread. In Northern India, Pakistan and Afghanistan, people will take their own dough to the baker who bakes the naan in a clay oven or* tandoor. *For a small fee he will stick the dough on the hot insides of the oven. The tandoor gives the best results, but because they're rare in Canada, I've given an alternative.*

| | | |
|---|---|---|
| 2 cups | all-purpose or whole wheat bread flour | 500 mL |
| ¼ tsp | quick-rising yeast | 1 mL |
| 1 tbsp | low-fat yogurt | 15 mL |
| ¼ tsp | salt | 1 mL |
| 1 tsp | sugar | 5 mL |
| 1 | small egg | 1 |
| ¼ tsp | baking powder | 1 mL |
| pinch | baking soda | pinch |
| ½ cup | water | 125 mL |
| ¼ cup | skim milk | 50 mL |
| | vegetable oil | |
| | dusting flour | |

1. Fold yeast into flour and set aside.
2. Mix remaining ingredients in blender, transfer to bowl and add flour-yeast mixture. Mix by hand or with dough mixer until dough is still sticky but comes away from sides of bowl. With hands, spread thin layer of vegetable oil over surface of dough to prevent drying. Cover with towel or plastic wrap and leave in warm place to rise for 4 to 6 hours.
3. Preheat oven to 500°F/260°C.
4. When dough has doubled in size, divide into 12 equal balls and roll out each to about ⅛ inch/3 mm thick. Place on non-stick baking pan and bake in middle of oven for 3 to 5 minutes or until firm to the touch. (If you want a tandoori effect, wet your fingers with water and touch a few spots on the rolled dough before baking. The naans will come out with crisp darkened spots where the water was.)

*Serves 4*

*Naan*

**If you make too many naans for your meal, just store them in the fridge for later use. You can toast them in the toaster if you just dampen them with wet hands. Naan can also be stuffed with salad or leftover vegetables for a tasty, nutritious lunch. Makes a great pizza crust too.**

**EACH SERVING PROVIDES:**

| | | |
|---|---|---|
| | Calories | 253 |
| g | Protein | 8 |
| g | Carbohydrates | 50 |
| g | Fibre | 2 |
| g | Fat | 2 |
| g | Saturated Fat | trace |
| mg | Cholesterol | 40 |
| mg | Sodium | 309 |
| mg | Potassium | 123 |

Excellent: thiamine
Good: riboflavin, niacin, iron

See photo, p. 85

# Fluffy Whole Wheat Flatbread

## PARATHA

*When people talk of Peshawar in Pakistan, two things come to mind: fragrant basmati rice and the fluffy paratha. Like a croissant, this bread gets its light texture from folding and re-rolling the dough to create layers.*

*For a flavour extra, sprinkle finely chopped ingredients on the dough after the first rolling. They will be incorporated into the dough when it's rolled again, and will cook briefly with the bread. Try some finely chopped browned onions, or a sprinkling of cilantro.*

*Indian Breads*

The flatbreads of India are not only food, they're eating utensils. For an informal meal, follow the Indian example and tear off a section of bread to scoop up a chunk of vegetable or meat in its sauce, with perhaps a bit of chutney or raita. Some Indian breads are now available in the refrigerated deli sections of supermarkets, but if you can't find them you can substitute pita bread, which now seems to be readily available everywhere.

| | | |
|---|---|---|
| 2 cups | whole wheat flour | 500 mL |
| 2 cups | all-purpose flour | 500 mL |
| ½ tsp | salt | 2 mL |
| 3 tbsp | vegetable oil | 45 mL |
| 2 cups | warm water | 500 mL |
| | vegetable oil spray | |

1. Combine flours and salt. Using hands or dough mixer, mix in 1 tbsp/15 mL of the oil. When oil is incorporated, add water and mix into sticky dough. Cover and leave for 30 minutes. (Keep remaining oil to brush on dough.)
2. Divide dough into 10 portions. Roll each into 12-inch/30 cm round. Use pastry brush to lightly spread each with some of remaining oil.
3. Dust 1 round with flour and slice from centre to edge. Lift one cut edge and roll into cone. Press cone flat, keeping point in centre. Roll again into 10-inch/25 cm round.
4. Spray heavy griddle or skillet with vegetable oil and wipe off excess. Heat over medium heat. Place dough in skillet and cook for 1 to 2 minutes. Flip over and lightly brush top with oil. Cook second side for 1 to 2 minutes and flip again. Lightly oil second side. Cook until both sides are golden brown. Serve immediately, or wrap several cooked parathas in foil and reheat in 300°F/150°C oven for 10 minutes or until warm.

*Serves 10*

**EACH SERVING PROVIDES:**

| | | |
|---|---|---|
| | Calories | 208 |
| g | Protein | 6 |
| g | Carbohydrates | 37 |
| g | Fibre | 4 |
| g | Fat | 5 |
| g | Saturated Fat | trace |
| mg | Cholesterol | 0 |
| mg | Sodium | 110 |
| mg | Potassium | 124 |

Good: thiamine, iron

# Ranjeet's Cornbread
## MAKKI KI ROTI

*My very loyal assistant, Ranjeet, showed me how to make this stovetop cornbread. I keep no secrets, so I'm happy to share this recipe with you. In my cooking classes I have tested and improved it over the years. A great accompaniment is spinach and Indian cheese (saag panir) on p. 50.*

| ¾ cup | water | 175 mL |
|---|---|---|
| 1 cup | corn flour | 250 mL |
| | vegetable oil | |
| | waxed paper squares, 6 inches/15 cm square | |

1. Boil water, then remove from heat. Sift corn flour into bowl and add water in steady stream while stirring. When mixture cools somewhat, knead in bowl for 3 to 4 minutes. (Rub some vegetable oil on hands to prevent dough from sticking.)
2. Divide dough into 4 equal baseball-sized balls. Place balls on waxed paper and press by hand to flatten. Press to ⅛-inch/3 mm thickness.
3. Cook each round separately. Spray heavy griddle or skillet with vegetable oil and wipe off excess. Heat over medium heat. Carefully place cornbread in skillet dough side down, and remove waxed paper. Turn when one side has brown spots, approximately 1½ minutes. Cook other side for 3 to 4 minutes.

*Serves 4*

**EACH SERVING PROVIDES:**

| | Calories | 104 |
|---|---|---|
| g | Protein | 3 |
| g | Carbohydrates | 22 |
| g | Fibre | 3 |
| g | Fat | 1 |
| g | Saturated Fat | trace |
| mg | Cholesterol | 0 |
| mg | Sodium | 3 |
| mg | Potassium | 85 |

Excellent: thiamine

# Simple Flatbread
## CHAPATI

*Chapati Fluffer*
**To get that authentic chapati look, bubbles and grill marks and all, you want to expose chapatis to direct heat. Indian shops carry a chapati fluffer—a wire-handled toasting rack that holds flatbreads over a gas burner or electric element for a few seconds to puff up. A cake rack placed over a burner or element set on high heat gives you the same effect. Turn the chapati quickly with tongs to avoid burning.**

**EACH SERVING PROVIDES:**

|   | Calories | 102 |
|---|---|---|
| g | Protein | 4 |
| g | Carbohydrates | 22 |
| g | Fibre | 3 |
| g | Fat | 1 |
| g | Saturated Fat | trace |
| mg | Cholesterol | 0 |
| mg | Sodium | 2 |
| mg | Potassium | 122 |

See photo, p. 84

*The chapati is the equivalent of the Mexican tortilla—as much an eating utensil as a bread. You may also know chapati as* roti, *the name it goes by in places like Fiji, Jamaica and Suriname. In Hindi, the national language of India, "roti" simply means "food" (food as in daily bread). Indians eat chapatis with dips, chutneys, pickles, omelettes, curries and just plain.*

| 1 cup | whole wheat flour | 250 mL |
|---|---|---|
| ½ cup | water | 125 mL |
|  | dusting flour |  |
|  | vegetable oil spray |  |

1. Combine ingredients by hand to form dough. Knead dough until sticky. (A bit of vegetable oil rubbed on your hands keeps dough from sticking.) Let rest 10 minutes so moisture is evenly distributed.
2. Knead well until dough is elastic. Let dough sit for 10 to 15 minutes.
3. Divide dough into 4 equal balls. Press down, dust with flour and roll with rolling pin. Try to roll into 8-inch/20 cm rounds.
4. Spray heavy skillet with vegetable oil and wipe off excess with paper towel. Heat skillet over medium-high heat and cook each round separately. When bubbles start rising on top, about 40 seconds, turn over to cook other side for about 30 seconds.

*Makes 4 chapatis*

# Chickpea Pancake
## CHILLA

*When I was young, my mother would not allow me or my sisters and brothers to eat food from the street vendors. But that didn't stop us from the occasional visit to Mama Kibibi's chilla stall. Hers were so good I had to learn her secret. Now my whole family enjoys these pancakes, but I never did tell my mother who taught me the recipe.*

| | | |
|---|---|---|
| 2 cups | chickpea flour (channa flour) | 500 mL |
| 1 cup | water | 250 mL |
| 1 | egg | 1 |
| ½ tsp | crushed ginger | 2 mL |
| ½ tsp | crushed garlic | 2 mL |
| ½ tsp | red chili powder, or to taste | 2 mL |
| ½ tsp | minced green chili, or to taste | 2 mL |
| 1 tsp | chopped cilantro | 5 mL |
| 2 tsp | vegetable oil | 10 mL |

1. Sift chickpea flour into bowl. Combine water, egg, ginger, garlic, chili powder, minced chili and cilantro. Stir into flour until smooth. This should be like crepe batter: thin but not watery (add more water if needed).
2. Heat large heavy non-stick skillet over high heat with a drop of vegetable oil. With paper towel, wipe oil over bottom. Pour in just enough batter to thinly cover bottom of pan. Lift and flip when bubbles appear on top. Chilla cooks quickly—about 1½ minutes for first side, 30 seconds for reverse side. Repeat until all batter is gone, separating pancakes with waxed paper. Pancakes can be reheated in a few seconds in microwave or frying pan. Serve hot or cold with coconut chutney (p. 108).

*Serves 8*

*Chickpea Flour*
*Channa flour, besan*
**Channa flour is a high-protein flour made of dried split chickpeas. It's too dense on its own to make bread, but can be added to enrich other bread recipes. Store this flour in the fridge or it will go rancid.**

**EACH SERVING PROVIDES:**

| | | |
|---|---|---|
| | Calories | 121 |
| g | Carbohydrates | 22 |
| g | Fibre | 4 |
| g | Protein | 5 |
| g | Fat | 2 |
| g | Saturated Fat | trace |
| mg | Cholesterol | 23 |
| mg | Sodium | 11 |
| mg | Potassium | 134 |

# Steamed Rice Bread

## IDLI

*Idli and chutney is Indian snack food. It can be used as dumplings with soup. It also makes a nice light lunch, or even breakfast, when served with sambar (p. 10), the thick lentil vegetable soup that's a staple in India. Idli and the stuffed crepes called masala dosa (p. 44) are eaten in the South of India the way eggs, bacon and sausage are here. If you don't have time to make them from scratch, check in Indian grocery stores, where you can find a commercial mix that makes idli and dosas. Idli also freezes well.*

| | | |
|---|---|---|
| 1½ cups | rice | 375 mL |
| ½ cup | lentils, preferably Indian black bean lentils (urad daal) | 125 mL |
| 1 tsp | fenugreek seeds | 5 mL |
| 1 cup | water | 250 mL |
| 1 tsp | Eno Effervescing Powder or double-acting baking powder | 5 mL |

1. Mix rice, lentils and fenugreek seeds and soak in 1 cup/250 mL water for 2 to 8 hours. Do not drain.
2. Grind or blend to smooth paste. Leave in warm place to ferment for 12 hours.
3. Add some water to bring to thick pancake batter consistency.
4. Lightly oil egg-poaching cups or small custard cups. In steamer heat water. Add Eno Effervescing Powder to mixture and beat well. Pour into cups and place in steamer. (Recipe makes 10. Add Eno only to what you're going to cook immediately.)
5. Steam for 15 minutes. Or microwave on high power in batches of 4 for no more than 4 minutes. Serve with thick lentil vegetable soup (p. 10) or coconut chutney (p. 108).

*Serves 10 as appetizer*

---

*Eno*

**You won't find Eno Antacid Effervescing Powder in the baking section of your store. Look for it in the pharmacy.**

**Eno is an antacid, but all over India people use it when they need a rising agent that acts immediately. In any dish that calls for Eno, have everything ready to go before you add it, then cook right away. Double-acting baking powder works quickly as well, and can be used as a substitute.**

**EACH SERVING PROVIDES:**

| | | |
|---|---|---|
| | Calories | 144 |
| g | Protein | 5 |
| g | Carbohydrates | 30 |
| g | Fibre | 2 |
| g | Fat | trace |
| g | Saturated Fat | trace |
| mg | Cholesterol | 0 |
| mg | Sodium | 74 |
| mg | Potassium | 90 |
| Good: folacin | | |

# Pickles, Chutneys, Dips and Sauces

*indicates hot dishes*

# Instant Carrot Pickle

*Some pickles take days or weeks to be ready to serve, but this one's ready immediately. It's a good accompaniment to any dish.*

| | | |
|---|---|---|
| 2 cups | carrots, cooking apples, underripe papaya or combination, peeled | 500 mL |
| 1 tsp | Dijon mustard | 5 mL |
| ½ tsp | Dhania-jeera Masala (p. 6) or mild curry powder | 2 mL |
| ¼ tsp | ground turmeric | 1 mL |
| ¼ tsp | red chili powder | 1 mL |
| ½ tsp | lemon juice | 2 mL |
| ½ tsp | vinegar | 2 mL |
| ½ tsp | salt | 2 mL |

1. Cut carrots or fruit into 1-inch long/2.5 cm matchstick pieces.
2. Combine spices and add carrots or fruit. Mix until evenly coated. Will keep in fridge for 2 to 3 days.

*Makes 30 1-tbsp/15 mL servings*

**EACH SERVING PROVIDES:**

| | | |
|---|---|---|
| | Calories | 6 |
| g | Protein | trace |
| g | Carbohydrates | 1 |
| g | Fibre | trace |
| g | Fat | trace |
| g | Saturated Fat | trace |
| mg | Cholesterol | 0 |
| mg | Sodium | 47 |
| mg | Potassium | 27 |

Excellent: vitamin A

# Quick Vegetable Pickle
### SAMBHARO

*Sambharo is another quick pickle. It's a good accompaniment to pulao (p. 23) or any other rice dish. This pickle will keep in a covered bowl in the fridge for approximately 2 weeks. Or, freeze it if you make too much.*

| | | |
|---|---|---|
| 1 cup | underripe papaya or tart cooking apple, peeled, sliced 1 inch/2.5 cm thick | 250 mL |
| 1 cup | carrots, peeled, sliced 1 inch/2.5 cm thick | 250 mL |
| 1 cup | cabbage, sliced 1 inch/2.5 cm thick | 250 mL |
| 1 to 2 | green chilies (or to taste), finely sliced | 1 to 2 |
| 1 | green or red pepper, diced | 1 |
| 1 tbsp | oil | 15 mL |
| ½ tsp | mustard seeds | 2 mL |
| ½ tsp | cumin seeds | 2 mL |
| | a few curry leaves, optional | |
| 1 tsp | ground turmeric | 5 mL |
| ½ tsp | crushed ginger | 2 mL |
| ½ tsp | crushed garlic | 2 mL |
| 1 tsp | salt | 5 mL |
| 2 tsp | sugar | 10 mL |
| 1 tbsp | chickpea flour (channa flour) | 15 mL |
| 2 tbsp | lemon juice | 25 mL |

1. Combine first 5 ingredients.
2. Heat oil in wok or skillet over high heat. Add mustard and cumin seeds. When seeds start to pop, add curry leaves and vegetable-fruit mixture. Add ground turmeric, ginger, garlic, salt and sugar and stir-fry for 10 minutes.
3. When vegetables are tender, sprinkle with chickpea flour and lemon juice. Reduce heat to low and cook, stirring, for another 5 minutes.

*Makes 50 1–tbsp/15 mL servings*

*Quick Reduction*
**To reduce a sauce quickly and keep the colours and flavours brighter, use the widest possible pan and boil over high heat. The moisture evaporates more quickly from the larger surface.**

EACH SERVING PROVIDES:

| | | |
|---|---|---|
| | Calories | 8 |
| g | Protein | trace |
| g | Carbohydrates | 1 |
| g | Fibre | trace |
| g | Fat | trace |
| g | Saturated Fat | trace |
| mg | Cholesterol | 0 |
| mg | Sodium | 45 |
| mg | Potassium | 30 |

Excellent: vitamin A

# Fresh Mango Chutney

*This uncooked chutney can be used as a bright-flavoured salsa to add sparkle to a plain grilled piece of fish, chicken or meat. It's also a good accompaniment to rice, curry and bread of any sort.*

| | | |
|---|---|---|
| 2 | underripe mangoes or peaches or tart apples | 2 |
| 2 tsp | wine vinegar | 10 mL |
| 2 tbsp | chopped roasted cashew nuts | 25 mL |
| 1 | red chili, seeded and sliced | 1 |
| ½ tsp | crushed dried mint | 2 mL |
| ¼ tsp | red chili powder | 1 mL |
| ½ tsp | ground cumin | 2 mL |
| ½ tsp | ground coriander | 2 mL |
| | mint leaves for garnish | |

1. Peel and seed fruit and slice thinly.
2. Combine vinegar, cashews, sliced chili, crushed mint and mangoes. Mix well.
3. Mix chili powder with cumin and coriander. Sprinkle over mango mixture and refrigerate for a couple of hours.
4. Before serving, stir fruit to coat with spices. Garnish with mint leaves.

*Makes 20 1-tbsp/15 mL servings*

**EACH SERVING PROVIDES:**

| | | |
|---|---|---|
| | Calories | 20 |
| g | Protein | trace |
| g | Carbohydrates | 4 |
| g | Fibre | 1 |
| g | Fat | 1 |
| g | Saturated Fat | trace |
| mg | Cholesterol | 0 |
| mg | Sodium | 7 |
| mg | Potassium | 48 |

Excellent: vitamin A, vitamin C

# Sweet Mango Chutney

*Mango chutney is commonly known as* murabba. *Generally I prefer my chutney hot, but I eat this the way North Americans eat jam.*

| | | |
|---|---|---|
| 1½ lb | peeled slightly underripe mangoes or tart apples or drained canned pineapple | 750 g |
| 1 | clove garlic, minced | 1 |
| 1 tbsp | chopped ginger | 15 mL |
| ½ cup | orange juice | 125 mL |
| ½ tsp | ground cinnamon or 2-inch/5 cm stick | 2 mL |
| pinch | ground cloves or 2 cloves, crushed | pinch |
| ½ tsp | salt | 2 mL |
| ¼ cup | sugar | 50 mL |
| 1 cup | cider vinegar | 250 mL |
| ¼ tsp | Chili Paste (p. 90) or minced chili (optional) | 1 mL |

1. Peel, seed and coarsely chop fruit.
2. Combine all ingredients in large non-aluminum pot and bring to boil. Reduce heat to medium and simmer for 1 hour.
3. Sterilize glass sealing jars in large pot of boiling water. Pour boiling water over lids in metal bowl or pot, and allow to sit for 3 minutes. Place jars upside down on clean towel to dry. Fill jars to ¼ inch/5 mm from top with chutney, wipe jar tops clean and attach lids. Lids will seal as chutney cools. Chutney will keep 1 year in sealed jars.

*Makes 50 1-tbsp/15 mL servings*

### Mangoes

**An Indian garden might have several varieties of mango trees for an almost year-round supply. Mangoes are used in chutneys, pickles and desserts. They're used either green (see facing page) or ripe, depending on the purpose. In North America the closest equivalent is peaches, but in chutneys almost any fruit with a good balance of acid and sweetness will do.**

| EACH SERVING PROVIDES: | | |
|---|---|---|
| | Calories | 26 |
| g | Protein | trace |
| g | Carbohydrates | 7 |
| g | Fibre | trace |
| g | Fat | trace |
| g | Saturated Fat | trace |
| mg | Cholesterol | 0 |
| mg | Sodium | 22 |
| mg | Potassium | 33 |

# Coconut Chutney

*Coconut chutney is eaten with almost anything South Indian, but who ever thought you'd find coconut in a HeartSmart cookbook? Coconuts are one of the few plant foods with saturated fat. I've adapted this so it has that lovely coconut flavour without much saturated fat.*

*This goes well with steamed rice cakes (idli) (p. 102) and potato-stuffed crepes (masala dosa) (p. 44).*

| ½ cup | fine unsweetened coconut | 125 mL |
|---|---|---|
| 1 cup | water | 250 mL |
| 1 tsp | toasted lentils, preferably urad daal (optional) | 5 mL |
| 4 | green chilies, or to taste | 4 |
| ½ tsp | salt | 2 mL |
| 2 tbsp | yogurt | 25 mL |
| ½ cup | cilantro | 125 mL |
| 1 tsp | vegetable oil | 5 mL |
| ½ tsp | mustard seeds | 2 mL |
| | a few curry leaves (optional) | |

1. Add coconut and water to blender and soak coconut for 10 minutes. Add toasted lentils, green chilies, salt, yogurt and cilantro. Blend to slightly gritty consistency and put in bowl. Keep aside.
2. Heat oil in small pan. Add mustard seeds. As they start popping, add curry leaves. Remove from heat and add to coconut mixture. Mix well. Keeps 3 to 4 days if refrigerated.

*Makes 35 1-tbsp/15 mL servings*

**EACH SERVING PROVIDES:**

| | Calories | 12 |
|---|---|---|
| g | Protein | trace |
| g | Carbohydrates | 1 |
| g | Fibre | trace |
| g | Fat | 1 |
| g | Saturated Fat | 1 |
| mg | Cholesterol | trace |
| mg | Sodium | 31 |
| mg | Potassium | 28 |

Good: vitamin C

From top: Fruit-flavoured Iced Tea (p. 124), Tandoori Chicken (barbecued) (p. 84)

# Tamarind Chutney

*Tamarind chutney is worth making because it's so versatile. It goes particu-
larly well with tandoori dishes, but is delicious with many others as well.
Use it with the spiced salads called* chaats *(pp. 14–15), or as a barbecue sauce.*

| | | |
|---|---|---|
| 8 oz | package tamarind paste | 227 g |
| 2 cups | hot water for soaking | 500 mL |
| ½ cup | sugar | 125 mL |
| ¼ cup | water | 50 mL |
| 1 tbsp | salt | 15 mL |
| 2 tbsp | red chili powder, or to taste | 25 mL |

1. Soak tamarind paste in hot water for 2 hours. Place tamarind and soaking
   liquid in blender and blend slowly (do not crush seeds). Strain into bowl
   through coarse-mesh sieve to remove seeds. Set aside.
2. Bring sugar and the ¼ cup water to boil in non-aluminum pot over high
   heat, and boil until dissolved. Add salt, chili powder and tamarind. Goes
   well with most appetizers.

*Makes 40 1-tbsp/15 mL servings*

# Tamarind Sauce

*This is a sweeter, milder version of the chutney.*

1. Using tamarind chutney recipe, increase sugar to 1 cup/250 mL, reduce
   salt to 1 tsp/5 mL and reduce chili to 1 tsp/5 mL. Adjust sugar to taste
   and add 2 cups/500 mL water. Follow method for cooking. Final prod-
   uct will be liquid and can be used as salad dressing or sauce for grilled
   meat. Dilute with water to taste for a refreshing tamarind drink. Use
   according to recipe in tamarind sherbet (p. 121).

*Makes 80 1-tbsp/15 mL servings*

Rose Milk Pudding (p. 117)

---

**Tamarind**

**The pulp from the pods
of the tamarind tree is used
to impart a gentle sourness
in Indian cooking.
Compressed tamarind
paste is convenient and
long lasting. Looking much
like bricks of compressed
dates, 8-ounce/227 g
packages are available in
Indian and Asian stores.**

**EACH SERVING PROVIDES:**

| | | |
|---|---|---|
| | Calories | 11 |
| g | Protein | trace |
| g | Carbohydrates | 3 |
| g | Fibre | trace |
| g | Fat | trace |
| g | Saturated Fat | trace |
| mg | Cholesterol | 0 |
| mg | Sodium | 48 |
| mg | Potassium | 10 |

**EACH SERVING PROVIDES:**

| | | |
|---|---|---|
| | Calories | 10 |
| g | Protein | trace |
| g | Carbohydrates | 3 |
| g | Fibre | trace |
| g | Fat | trace |
| g | Saturated Fat | trace |
| mg | Cholesterol | 0 |
| mg | Sodium | 26 |
| mg | Potassium | 2 |

See photo facing p. 37

# Kidney Bean Dip

**EACH SERVING PROVIDES:**

|  | Calories | 66 |
|---|---|---|
| g | Protein | 5 |
| g | Carbohydrates | 11 |
| g | Fibre | 4 |
| g | Fat | trace |
| g | Saturated Fat | trace |
| mg | Cholesterol | 1 |
| mg | Sodium | 9 |
| mg | Potassium | 223 |

Excellent: folacin

*A little dip and some naan bread or a chapati becomes a tasty appetizer or a very satisfying breakfast (and a lower-fat alternative to peanut butter). When you use fava beans instead of kidney beans and add olive oil, this becomes a Turkish phoul.*

| 1 cup | canned, drained kidney beans | 250 mL |
|---|---|---|
| ½ cup | cilantro, coarsely chopped | 125 mL |
| 2 | cloves garlic, coarsely chopped | 2 |
| ¼ tsp | ground cumin | 1 mL |
| 2 to 3 tbsp | low-fat yogurt | 25 to 45 mL |
| 1 tsp | lemon juice | 5 mL |

1. Rinse beans to remove excess salt. In food processor, combine all ingredients (including beans) and blend until smooth. Serve with pita or naan bread (p. 97).

*Serves 4*

# Chickpea Dip

### Canned Beans

**Beans have something for everyone. Vegetarians value them for the protein they provide, and they're a good fibre boost for non-vegetarians.**

**Canned beans are convenient to have on hand when you're too busy or in a rush and can't prepare ahead of time. If you use canned beans, make sure you rinse them well before you use them. They're usually high in salt.**

*Here's another dip with relatives in the Middle East. Add tahini (sesame paste) to this and it becomes the Greek hummos. A good idea works in any language.*

| 14 oz | tin chickpeas | 398 g |
|---|---|---|
| bunch | cilantro (fist-sized) | bunch |
| 2 to 4 | cloves garlic | 2 to 4 |
| 1 | small green pepper | 1 |
| 1 cup | yogurt | 250 mL |
| 3 to 4 | green onions | 3 to 4 |

1. Rinse chickpeas and drain. Wash cilantro and blot dry with towel or in salad spinner.

2. Combine chickpeas in food processor with garlic, pepper, yogurt and half the cilantro. Blend to paste.
3. Finely chop green onions and remaining cilantro and fold into mixture. Serve with pita or naan bread (p. 97).

*Serves 8*

# Cilantro Spread

*At home, we spread this on toast to replace butter, jam, peanut butter, avocado or cheese spreads. I serve this with bread for Sunday breakfasts. My family likes it a little hotter, so I add a pinch of red chili powder when cooking. With or without the chili, it's a treat any day of the week.*

| | | |
|---|---|---|
| bunch | cilantro (fist-sized) | bunch |
| 1 | medium tomato, quartered | 1 |
| 1 to 2 | cloves garlic | 1 to 2 |
| pinch | salt | pinch |
| 1 to 2 tsp | lemon juice | 5 to 10 mL |
| 1 tsp | vegetable oil | 5 mL |

1. Wash cilantro well to remove grit. Dry in salad spinner or blot dry. In food processor, combine cilantro, tomato, garlic, salt, lemon juice, then chop finely.
2. Heat oil in large non-stick skillet over high heat. Add chopped mixture. Cook, stirring, for about 2 minutes to reduce to paste consistency. This spread is good to eat fresh, but will keep for one week in the fridge in an airtight container.

*Serves 2*

**EACH SERVING PROVIDES:**

| | | |
|---|---|---|
| | Calories | 207 |
| g | Protein | 12 |
| g | Carbohydrates | 34 |
| g | Fibre | 6 |
| g | Fat | 4 |
| g | Saturated Fat | 1 |
| mg | Cholesterol | 2 |
| mg | Sodium | 35 |
| mg | Potassium | 555 |

Excellent: folacin
Good: thiamine, vitamin B-6, vitamin E, iron, zinc

**EACH SERVING PROVIDES:**

| | | |
|---|---|---|
| | Calories | 38 |
| g | Protein | 1 |
| g | Carbohydrates | 4 |
| g | Fibre | 1 |
| g | Fat | 3 |
| g | Saturated Fat | trace |
| mg | Cholesterol | 0 |
| mg | Sodium | 396 |
| mg | Potassium | 192 |

# Savoury Yogurt Sauce
## RAITA

*Low-fat Thick Yogurt*
**The longer you drain yogurt, the thicker it will get. Start with a low- or nonfat unflavoured yogurt with no gelatine or other thickeners.**

**Pour yogurt into cheese-cloth-lined sieve and cover with cloth. Place weight on top to press and put sieve in sink or large pan to catch liquid. Or, put yogurt into paper coffee filter in its plastic holder and use coffee-pot to catch liquid. Yogurt will be reduced by half in 1 hour.**

*You'll find* raita *all over India, and at every meal. Not only is it the best condiment on earth to put out the fire in your mouth from spicy dishes, it complements the flavour of any dish you serve it with. Raita also makes a nice salad dressing or dip.*

| | | |
|---|---|---|
| 2 cups | **Low-fat Thick Yogurt (see sidebar)** | 500 mL |
| ½ | **cucumber, seeded if necessary** | ½ |
| 1 | **carrot** | 1 |
| 1 tsp | **salt** | 5 mL |
| 1 tsp | **ground cumin** | 5 mL |
| 1 tsp | **sugar** | 5 mL |
| | **chopped mint or pinch dried ground mint** | |

1. Grate carrots and cucumber. Place in sieve and press to squeeze out as much moisture as possible.
2. Stir together all ingredients in large bowl. Seal bowl with plastic wrap and place in fridge to chill. Serve cold or at room temperature. If it weeps, simply stir before serving.

*Makes 20 2-tbsp/25 mL servings*

**EACH SERVING PROVIDES:**

| | | |
|---|---|---|
| | Calories | 17 |
| g | Protein | 2 |
| g | Carbohydrates | 3 |
| g | Fibre | trace |
| g | Fat | trace |
| g | Saturated Fat | trace |
| mg | Cholesterol | 1 |
| mg | Sodium | 104 |
| mg | Potassium | 68 |

See photos facing pp. 13, 85

# Indian Sweets & Drinks

# Almond Fudge

## BADAM BURFEE

*It's all a matter of budget. In Delhi, they use cashew nuts because they're more expensive than almonds; in East Africa, they use peanuts because they're cheaper than almonds. I use almonds because, regardless of price, they're my favourite.*

| ¾ cup | sugar | 175 mL |
|---|---|---|
| ½ cup | water | 125 mL |
| 2 cups | ground almonds or cashews or peanuts | 500 mL |
| 1 tsp | vanilla extract | 5 mL |
| ½ tsp | ground cardamom | 2 mL |
| 1 tbsp | 1% milk | 15 mL |
| 1 tbsp | unsalted butter | 15 mL |
| | vegetable oil spray | |

1. In heavy-bottomed pot, bring sugar and water to boil over high heat until soft ball stage (drop forms a soft ball when put into cold water; 234 to 240°F/110 to 115°C on candy thermometer). Add almonds, vanilla, cardamom and milk and cook, stirring, for 5 minutes or until mixture leaves sides of pot. Stir in butter with wooden spoon and remove from heat.
2. Lightly oil 8-by-8-inch/2 L cake pan with vegetable oil spray. Pour mixture into pan and press flat. Use sharp knife to cut into 30 pieces before cooling. Allow to cool at room temperature and remove pieces to an airtight container. Fudge will keep 12 to 20 days.

*Serves 30*

**EACH SERVING PROVIDES:**

| | Calories | 81 |
|---|---|---|
| g | Protein | 2 |
| g | Carbohydrates | 7 |
| g | Fibre | 1 |
| g | Fat | 5 |
| g | Saturated Fat | 1 |
| mg | Cholesterol | trace |
| mg | Sodium | 7 |
| mg | Potassium | 76 |

# Carrot Halva

*It can be difficult to find tasty HeartSmart desserts. My father had a sweet tooth and my mother wanted to keep him healthy. She gave me this recipe when she was visiting me a year ago (just in time for the book). You can decorate this sweet by pressing raisins into it.*

|            | vegetable oil spray            |        |
|------------|--------------------------------|--------|
| 1½ cups    | grated carrots (6 or 7 large carrots) | 375 mL |
| ½ cup      | sugar                          | 125 mL |
| 1 tsp      | unsalted butter                | 5 mL   |

1. Steam grated carrots in vegetable steamer or microwave until tender.
2. Lightly coat non-stick 8-inch/20 cm square pan with vegetable oil spray.
3. Place heavy-bottomed pot over high heat. Add sugar and steamed carrots. Cook, stirring constantly, for about 15 minutes. Do not let carrots stick to pot. When mixture comes away from sides of pot, stir in butter with wooden spoon. Remove from heat and press mixture into pan. Cut in 16 pieces before mixture cools. Use within 2 days.

*Serves 8*

**EACH SERVING PROVIDES:**

|     | Calories      | 84  |
|-----|---------------|-----|
| g   | Protein       | 1   |
| g   | Carbohydrates | 19  |
| g   | Fibre         | 2   |
| g   | Fat           | 1   |
| g   | Saturated Fat | 1   |
| mg  | Cholesterol   | 3   |
| mg  | Sodium        | 33  |
| mg  | Potassium     | 204 |

Excellent: vitamin A

# Date Halva

*Energy bars took England by storm a few years ago. They were tasty but expensive. I was part of a group of Indian mothers who decided to create our own homemade ones instead, and we sold them at street celebrations for* Diwali, *the Festival of Lights. They were a big hit. Dates were the secret. These energy bars are a natural alternative to toffee or candy of any sort.*

| | | |
|---|---|---|
| 7-oz pkg | pitted dates | 200 g |
| 1 tsp | unsalted butter | 5 mL |
| 1 tbsp | almonds | 15 mL |
| 1 tbsp | pistachio nuts (shelled) | 15 mL |
| 1 tsp | fine unsweetened coconut | 5 mL |

**2 sheets waxed paper
about 10 inches/25 cm square**

1. Warm dates in small pan over very low heat until softened. (Stir once or twice to ensure even heating.) Meanwhile, cut almonds into 8 pieces. Cut pistachio nuts in half.
2. Puree dates in food processor until supple, like dough.
3. Brush 1 sheet waxed paper with butter. Spread dates on paper and flatten. Place other sheet on top of dates. With rolling pin, press dates to spread evenly. Lift top sheet and evenly spread almond and pistachio nuts over top. Cover with top sheet and roll again. Remove from paper and roll dates into tube. Roll tube in coconut and wrap in waxed paper. Cut in half crosswise and place in fridge to set.
4. This recipe yields two 5-inch/12.5 cm rolls 1 inch/2.5 cm in diameter. When cold, slice into wheels ¼ inch/.5 cm thick to serve.

*Serves 10*

**EACH SERVING PROVIDES:**

| | | |
|---|---|---|
| | Calories | 69 |
| g | Protein | 1 |
| g | Carbohydrates | 15 |
| g | Fibre | 2 |
| g | Fat | 1 |
| g | Saturated Fat | trace |
| mg | Cholesterol | 1 |
| mg | Sodium | 5 |
| mg | Potassium | 146 |

# Rose Milk Pudding

## FALUDA

*Rose water, the diluted essence of rose petals, imparts a subtle, delicious flavour and, naturally enough, a lovely fragrance. You can buy it in bottles at Asian stores, supermarkets and even pharmacies. Or, use your favourite liqueur!*

*Some cooked vermicelli strands in a sugar syrup coloured red make for a nice presentation.*

| | | |
|---|---|---|
| 3 cups | 1% milk | 750 mL |
| 13 oz | tin evaporated skim milk | 385 mL |
| 1 or 2 drops | food colour (pink or green or yellow) | 1 or 2 drops |
| ⅛ tsp | rose water (7 drops) | 0.5 mL |
| ⅛ tsp | vanilla extract (7 drops) | 0.5 mL |
| 6 | cardamom seeds | 6 |
| ¾ cup | sugar | 175 mL |
| ⅓ oz | fresh agar (⅕ package) | 10 g |
| | or 2 tbsp/15 mL unflavoured gelatine | |
| 1 cup | water | 250 mL |
| 1 tsp | cornstarch | 5 mL |

1. In heavy-bottomed pot, combine fresh milk, evaporated milk, food colour, rose water, vanilla extract, cardamom and sugar and bring to boil. Boil for 15 minutes until reduced by about 20%.
2. Meanwhile, mix cornstarch with a little cold water. Rinse agar and soak in 1 cup/250 mL water. Place in microwave and heat on high until agar has dissolved completely (about 5 minutes) or pour 1 cup/250 ml boiling water over agar and let sit until dissolved. Or, for gelatine, sprinkle powder over ½ cup/125 mL cold water and let stand 1 minute. Add ½ cup/100 mL boiling water and stir until dissolved.
3. Add agar (or gelatine) and cornstarch to milk mixture. Cook for 5 to 10 more minutes until thickening begins. Lift out cardamom seeds if you wish. Remove from heat and whisk or blend. Pour into large serving bowl (or 8 single-portion moulds). Refrigerate until firm, at least 3 hours.
4. Serve cold. Run knife around edges of pudding and unmould, or spoon onto plates from large bowl. Pudding will keep covered in refrigerator for 4 to 5 days.

*Serves 8*

*Agar*
*China grass, faluda grass, Bengal isinglass*
**Agar is a natural thickening agent made from seaweed. It acts like the gelatine derived from animal sources (though it tastes different) because it contains the same protein. Agar has stronger setting properties than the unflavoured gelatine used in North America, so if you substitute gelatine, use about twice as much. Agar comes in two forms: fresh agar which comes in strands in 50 g packages, and powdered. Powdered agar has stronger jelling properties than fresh.**

**EACH SERVING PROVIDES:**

| | | |
|---|---|---|
| | Calories | 148 |
| g | Protein | 6 |
| g | Carbohydrates | 29 |
| g | Fibre | trace |
| g | Fat | 1 |
| g | Saturated Fat | 1 |
| mg | Cholesterol | 5 |
| mg | Sodium | 96 |
| mg | Potassium | 294 |

Excellent: vitamin D
Good: vitamin B-12, calcium

See photo facing p. 109

# Fruit Yogurt Delight

*My elder son has a taste for rich desserts, but this lower-fat concoction has the rich taste he loves without the fat.*

| | | |
|---|---|---|
| 2 tbsp | 1% milk | 25 mL |
| pinch | saffron | pinch |
| 1 tsp | crushed cardamom seeds | 5 mL |
| 1 tbsp | unsalted butter | 15 mL |
| 3 tbsp | brown sugar | 45 mL |
| ½ tsp | ground cinnamon | 2 mL |
| 4 | bananas, sliced | 4 |
| 3 cups | Low-fat Thick Yogurt (see p. 112) | 750 mL |
| 2 tbsp | honey | 25 mL |
| 2 tbsp | almond flakes | 25 mL |

1. In small heavy pot over high heat, bring milk, saffron and cardamom to boil. Boil for 10 minutes and remove from heat to cool.
2. Heat butter in non-stick skillet over high heat. Add sugar and cinnamon, then bananas. Cook bananas to caramelize. Remove from heat and place bananas in 8 serving dishes.
3. Add yogurt and honey to cooled milk mixture. Mix well. Spoon over bananas. Garnish with almond flakes. Chill and serve.

*Serves 8*

**EACH SERVING PROVIDES:**

| | | |
|---|---|---|
| | Calories | 166 |
| g | Protein | 6 |
| g | Carbohydrates | 28 |
| g | Fibre | 1 |
| g | Fat | 4 |
| g | Saturated Fat | 1 |
| mg | Cholesterol | 6 |
| mg | Sodium | 69 |
| mg | Potassium | 477 |

Excellent: vitamin B-12
Good: riboflavin, vitamin B-6, calcium

# Rice Pudding
## KHEER

*Many people in England grow up with institutional rice pudding, and some learn to loathe it, but once they taste my version of it, most of them are moved to change their minds.*

| | | |
|---|---|---|
| ½ cup | pudding rice or any short-grain rice | 125 mL |
| 3 cups | water | 750 mL |
| 2 cups | 1% milk | 500 mL |
| 13-oz | tin evaporated skim milk | 385 mL |
| 4 tbsp | sugar | 60 mL |
| pinch | saffron | pinch |
| 6 to 8 | cardamom seeds | 6 to 8 |
| | | |
| 1 tsp | almond flakes | 5 mL |
| 1 tsp | grated unsalted pistachio nuts | 5 mL |

1. Rinse rice and soak for 15 minutes. Drain. Boil in 3 cups/750 mL water until tender.
2. Combine fresh milk and evaporated milk and bring to boil in heavy non-stick pan over high heat. Stir often.
3. Add sugar, saffron and cardamom and simmer for 30 minutes, stirring occasionally. When milk has thickened, add boiled rice and thicken a little more.
4. Pour into serving dish and garnish with almond flakes and grated pistachio nuts. Refrigerate to chill. Serve cold.

*Serves 6*

**EACH SERVING PROVIDES:**

| | | |
|---|---|---|
| | Calories | 180 |
| g | Protein | 8 |
| g | Carbohydrates | 31 |
| g | Fibre | 1 |
| g | Fat | 2 |
| g | Saturated Fat | 1 |
| mg | Cholesterol | 5 |
| mg | Sodium | 107 |
| mg | Potassium | 349 |

Excellent: vitamin D

Good: vitamin B-12, calcium

# Saffron Cream
## SHRIKHAND

*The subcontinent of India started its life attached to Africa, then drifted up to its present location. The impact created the Himalayas. Shrikhand is the Sanskrit word for the Indian subcontinent, and what a tribute to the wonders of this accident of continental drift.*

*There's no cream in this rich, silky, special-occasion dessert, but you'd never know it. For an everyday dessert you can leave out the saffron. Eat it on its own or with a tropical fruit salad.*

| | | |
|---|---|---|
| 4 cups | Low-fat Thick Yogurt (p. 112) | 1 L |
| ½ cup | superfine sugar (or granulated sugar pulsed in blender) | 125 mL |
| ¼ tsp | ground cardamom | 1 mL |
| 1 tsp | 1% milk | 5 mL |
| pinch | saffron strands | pinch |
| 1 tsp | crushed pistachio nuts | 5 mL |
| 1 tsp | crushed almond | 5 mL |

1. Beat together yogurt and sugar. Add cardamom and mix well.
2. Warm milk and add saffron strands. When milk turns yellow, gently fold into yogurt mixture. Press into container, cover and refrigerate to cool. To serve, scoop into bowls with ice cream scoop and garnish with nuts.

*Serves 8*

**EACH SERVING PROVIDES:**

| | | |
|---|---|---|
| | Calories | 233 |
| g | Protein | 14 |
| g | Carbohydrates | 35 |
| g | Fibre | trace |
| g | Fat | 4 |
| g | Saturated Fat | 3 |
| mg | Cholesterol | 16 |
| mg | Sodium | 182 |
| mg | Potassium | 613 |

Excellent: riboflavin, vitamin B-12, calcium, zinc

# Tamarind Sherbet

*I gave this recipe to our Italian friend who makes 180 flavours of ice cream. I now supply him with all the tamarind sauce he needs for his sherbet, which he makes for some very prestigious hotel dining rooms.*

| ½ cup | skim milk | 125 mL |
| 4 tsp | sugar | 20 mL |
| 2 cups | ice | 500 mL |
| 3 to 4 tsp | Tamarind Sauce (p. 109) | 15 to 20 mL |

1. In blender, blend milk and sugar. Add ice and tamarind sauce and blend some more until ice is completely crushed. Serve immediately.
   Or, for granita-style presentation, put blender mixture in small cake pan and place in freezer for a few hours. Stir with fork every half hour to break up ice crystals and prevent it from freezing solid. Texture will be like grainy snow.

*Serves 4*

**EACH SERVING PROVIDES:**

| | Calories | 28 |
|---|---|---|
| g | Protein | 1 |
| g | Carbohydrates | 6 |
| g | Fibre | trace |
| g | Fat | trace |
| g | Saturated Fat | trace |
| mg | Cholesterol | 1 |
| mg | Sodium | 41 |
| mg | Potassium | 52 |

# Indian Spiced Tea
## MASALA CHAI

Chai *means tea.* Masala chai *means spiced tea. You can brew tea by introducing whole spices and boiling, or use a ground blend. A coarse grind for spices is preferred because you don't want the powder to go through the tea strainer. Any good black tea works in chai, but green tea leaves are not suitable.*

| | | |
|---|---|---|
| 5 cups | water | 1.25 L |
| ¼ tsp | Spice Mix (see below) | 1 mL |
| 2 | 2-cup tea bags | 2 |
| 1 cup | 2% milk | 250 mL |
| 4 to 8 tsp | sugar to taste | 20 to 40 mL |

1. Boil water with spice mix. Reduce to 4 cups/1 L. Add tea bags and boil for a minute. Add milk and boil for 2 minutes. Remove tea bags. Add sugar and serve hot.

*Spice Mix:*

| | | |
|---|---|---|
| 1 tbsp | ground ginger | 15 mL |
| 1 tbsp | ground black pepper | 15 mL |
| 2 tsp | Garam Masala (page 6) | 10 mL |

1. Mix well.

*Serves 4*

**EACH SERVING PROVIDES:**

| | | |
|---|---|---|
| | Calories | 57 |
| g | Protein | 2 |
| g | Carbohydrates | 10 |
| g | Fibre | trace |
| g | Fat | 1 |
| g | Saturated Fat | 1 |
| mg | Cholesterol | 5 |
| mg | Sodium | 40 |
| mg | Potassium | 142 |

# Milk Delights

*A cooling milkshake on a summer day; a steaming mug of hot chocolate when it's cold outside—these are the Indian equivalents.*

*Winter*

| | | |
|---|---|---|
| 2 cups | 1% milk | 500 mL |
| 13-oz | tin evaporated skim milk | 385 mL |
| 2 tbsp | crushed almonds | 25 mL |
| 6 to 8 | cardamom seeds | 6 to 8 |
| | a few strands saffron | |
| 2 tbsp | sugar | 25 mL |

1. In heavy-bottomed pot over high heat, combine all ingredients, stir and bring to boil. Boil for 5 minutes and serve hot. You can strain if it you like, but it's rather nice to crunch down on a whole cardamom seed.

*Serves 4*

*Summer*

| | | |
|---|---|---|
| 3 cups | 1% milk | 750 mL |
| 2 cups | fruit (combination or any one of: mango, banana, raspberry, strawberry) | 500 mL |
| 3 tbsp | honey | 45 mL |
| pinch | ground cardamom | pinch |
| 5 to 6 | frozen cubes skim milk | 5 to 6 |

1. Blend all ingredients in blender. Serve cold. (You can start with frozen fruit or frozen milk cubes, whichever is easier. If you start with frozen fruit, use 3½ cups/875 mL milk)

*Serves 4*

EACH SERVING PROVIDES:

| | | |
|---|---|---|
| | Calories | 213 |
| g | Protein | 15 |
| g | Carbohydrates | 28 |
| g | Fibre | 1 |
| g | Fat | 5 |
| g | Saturated Fat | 1 |
| mg | Cholesterol | 9 |
| mg | Sodium | 209 |
| mg | Potassium | 665 |

Excellent: riboflavin, vitamin B-12, vitamin D, calcium

Good: vitamin A, vitamin E, zinc

EACH SERVING PROVIDES:

| | | |
|---|---|---|
| | Calories | 187 |
| g | Protein | 7 |
| g | Carbohydrates | 37 |
| g | Fibre | 1 |
| g | Fat | 2 |
| g | Saturated Fat | 1 |
| mg | Cholesterol | 8 |
| mg | Sodium | 105 |
| mg | Potassium | 461 |

Excellent: vitamin B-12, vitamin D,

Good: vitamin A, riboflavin, vitamin C, calcium

# Fruit-flavoured Iced Tea

*Fruit flavoured iced teas are now available in bottles and cans. This refreshing drink gives you an easy and inexpensive alternative to those ready-made teas.*

| | | |
|---|---|---|
| 2 cups | hot tea | 500 mL |
| 1 tbsp | sugar | 15 mL |
| 1 tsp | grated ginger | 5 mL |
| ½ tsp | dried mint, or some fresh leaves | 2 mL |
| ½ cup | orange juice | 125 mL |
| 2 tbsp | lemon juice | 25 mL |

1. Add sugar, ginger and mint to tea. Let stand until cold. Strain through fine-mesh sieve to remove solids. Add fruit juice to tea and pour over ice.

*Serves 4*

# Yogurt Drink
## LASSI

*Lassi is a yogurt shake. All over India you'll find it in different forms. In Punjab, people drink sweet lassi and fruit-flavoured lassi. In Gujarat and the South, it's savoury, with salt, cumin and mint. Some people add black pepper for the tang.*

*Sweet Lassi*

| | | |
|---|---|---|
| 1½ cups | low-fat plain yogurt | 375 mL |
| 8 tsp | sugar | 40 mL |
| 2 cups | ice cubes | 500 mL |

*Fruit Lassi*

| | | |
|---|---|---|
| 1½ cups | low-fat plain yogurt | 375 mL |
| 2 tbsp | sugar | 25 mL |
| ½ cup | crushed mango, raspberries or strawberries | 125 mL |
| 1½ cups | ice cubes | 375 mL |

*Salted Lassi*

| 1 cup | low-fat plain yogurt | 250 mL |
| pinch | salt | pinch |
| pinch | freshly toasted ground cumin | pinch |
| 1 cup | water | 250 mL |
| 1½ cups | ice cubes | 375 mL |

*Mint Lassi*

| 1 cup | low-fat plain yogurt | 250 mL |
| pinch | salt | pinch |
| pinch | freshly toasted ground cumin | pinch |
| 1 cup | water | 250 mL |
| 1½ cups | ice cubes | 375 mL |
| pinch | dried mint, or 1 finely chopped mint leaf | pinch |

1. Blend all ingredients in blender. Yields 12 ounces/175 mL of lassi.

*Serves 4*

**EACH SERVING PROVIDES:**

*(Salted Lassi)*

| | Calories | 36 |
| g | Protein | 3 |
| g | Carbohydrates | 4 |
| g | Fibre | trace |
| g | Fat | 1 |
| g | Saturated Fat | 1 |
| mg | Cholesterol | 3 |
| mg | Sodium | 335 |
| mg | Potassium | 135 |

Good: vitamin B-12

**EACH SERVING PROVIDES:**

*(Mint Lassi)*

| | Calories | 37 |
| g | Protein | 3 |
| g | Carbohydrates | 4 |
| g | Fibre | trace |
| g | Fat | 1 |
| g | Saturated Fat | 1 |
| mg | Cholesterol | 3 |
| mg | Sodium | 335 |
| mg | Potassium | 134 |

Good: vitamin B-12

See photos facing pp. 13, 108

125

# *Index*